Cambridge Eler

C000260424

Elements in Public and Nonprofit /
edited by
Andrew Whitford
University of Georgia
Robert Christensen
Brigham Young University

INSTITUTIONAL MEMORY AS STORYTELLING

How Networked Government Remembers

Jack Corbett
University of Southampton
Dennis C. Grube
University of Cambridge
Heather Lovell
University of Tasmania
Rodney James Scott
University of New South Wales

CAMBRIDGE
UNIVERSITY PRESS

CAMBRIDGE
UNIVERSITY PRESS

University Printing House, Cambridge CB2 8BS, United Kingdom

One Liberty Plaza, 20th Floor, New York, NY 10006, USA

477 Williamstown Road, Port Melbourne, VIC 3207, Australia

314–321, 3rd Floor, Plot 3, Splendor Forum, Jasola District Centre, New Delhi – 110025, India

79 Anson Road, #06–04/06, Singapore 079906

Cambridge University Press is part of the University of Cambridge.

It furthers the University's mission by disseminating knowledge in the pursuit of education, learning, and research at the highest international levels of excellence.

www.cambridge.org
Information on this title: www.cambridge.org/9781108748001
DOI: 10.1017/9781108780001

© Jack Corbett, Dennis C. Grube, Heather Lovell and Rodney James Scott 2020

This publication is in copyright. Subject to statutory exception and to the provisions of relevant collective licensing agreements, no reproduction of any part may take place without the written permission of Cambridge University Press.

First published 2020

A catalogue record for this publication is available from the British Library.

ISBN 978-1-108-74800-1 Paperback
ISSN 2515-4303 (online)
ISSN 2515-429X (print)

Cambridge University Press has no responsibility for the persistence or accuracy of URLs for external or third-party internet websites referred to in this publication and does not guarantee that any content on such websites is, or will remain, accurate or appropriate.

Institutional Memory as Storytelling

How Networked Government Remembers

Elements in Public and Nonprofit Administration

DOI: 10.1017/9781108780001
First published online: November 2020

Jack Corbett
University of Southampton

Dennis C. Grube
University of Cambridge

Heather Lovell
University of Tasmania

Rodney James Scott
University of New South Wales

Author for correspondence: Jack Corbett, j.corbett@soton.ac.uk

Abstract: How do bureaucracies remember? The conventional view is that institutional memory is static and singular, the sum of recorded files and learned procedures. There is a growing body of scholarship that suggests contemporary bureaucracies are failing at this core task. This Element argues that this diagnosis misses that memories are essentially dynamic stories. They reside with people and are thus dispersed across the array of actors that make up the differentiated polity. Drawing on four policy examples from four sectors (housing, energy, family violence and justice) in three countries (the UK, Australia and New Zealand), this Element argues that treating the way institutions remember as storytelling is both empirically salient and normatively desirable. It is concluded that the current conceptualisation of institutional memory needs to be recalibrated to fit the types of policy learning practices required by modern collaborative governance.

Keywords: institutional memory, networked governance, policy learning, storytelling

© Jack Corbett, Dennis C. Grube, Heather Lovell and Rodney James Scott 2020

ISBNs: 9781108748001 (PB), 9781108780001 (OC)
ISSNs: 2515-4303 (online), 2515-429X (print)

Contents

1 Introduction

Democratic governance is defined by the regular rotation of elected leaders. Amidst the churn, the civil service is expected to act as the repository of received wisdom about past policies, including assessments of what works and what doesn't (Richards and Smith 2016). The claim is that to avoid repeating the same mistakes we need to know what happened last time and what the effects were. Institutional memory is thus central to the pragmatic task of governing.

There is a growing body of scholarship that questions whether declining institutional memory allows modern bureaucracies to fulfil this function adequately (Pollitt 2000, 2007, 2008, 2009; Wettenhall 2011; Rhodes and Tiernan 2014; Lindquist and Eichbaum 2016; Stark 2019; Stark and Head 2019). The argument is that a decline in institutional memory has occurred against a background of wider changes in the governance environment, including the advent of new public management (NPM), digital transformation, the influence of ministerial advisers, the twenty-four-hour news cycle and its impact on the increasing pace of government, and changing 'bargains' between political executives and the bureaucracy (Marsh and Rhodes 1992; Rhodes 1997; Hood and Lodge 2006; Marsh 2011). Increasingly, scholars characterise policy change as being steered by networks, with the siloed workings of departments being dragged into more collaborative ways of working across government and in co-production with the private sector and community organisations (Osborne 2009; Alford and O'Flynn 2012; Bartenberger and Sześciło 2016).

In this new environment no single actor or organisation is capable of retaining the full *memory* of a process of which they were simply one part. Rather, *memories* are necessarily dispersed. The key question for both academics and policymakers is, how can institutional memory continue to be captured when it is distributed so widely? If past ways of institutionalising memory are no longer sufficient in the fast and continuous information flows required for modern governance, then we need conceptual tools capable of seeing memory as something more than simply a file stored in a single location.

In this Element, we argue that one of the key reasons why institutional memory has become problematic is that it has been conceptualised in a 'static' manner more in keeping with an older way of doing government. This practice has assumed that knowledge on a given topic is held centrally (by government departments) and can be made explicit for the purpose of archiving. But, if government doesn't work this way then we shouldn't expect it to remember this way either. Policymaking itself is messy and draws on many kinds of imperfect evidence (see Cairney 2016). Policy memory is equally messy. Instead of static repositories of summative documents holding a singular 'objective' memory, in this Element we propose a more 'dynamic' people-centred conceptualisation that sees institutional memory as a composite of intersubjective memories open to change. This draws to the fore the role of actors as crucial interpreters of memory, combining the documentary record with their own perspectives to create stories about the past.

What Is Institutional Memory?

The idea that memory is central to the task of governing is hardly new. Lindblom's (1959) model of 'muddling through' highlights that policies tend to be developed incrementally, and in this sense institutional memories are important for enabling 'tried and tested' policies from the past to resurface and, with small modifications, be used again. Similarly, there are now well-established theoretical perspectives on historical institutionalism and path dependency which argue that the past constrains the future (Pierson 2000, 2004; Bell 2011; Lowndes and Roberts 2013). The recent emergence of more actor-centred variants of institutionalism foreground the power of agents in creating change through ideas and discourse, giving shape to how individuals in government perceive their work (Schmidt 2008; Bevir and Rhodes 2010; Bell 2011; Hay 2011; Rhodes 2011). This has particular resonance for the study of institutional memory. Whether through the conscious agency of actors, or some more formalised organisational structure, what institutions remember affects the way they frame future tasks.

As this work illustrates, institutional memory has been implicitly central to the study of public administration for decades, but it is only recently that scholars have turned to its explicit study in a systematic way (Pollitt 2000, 2007, 2008, 2009; Wettenhall 2011; Rhodes and Tiernan 2014). This emerging literature has both empirical and normative aims. Empirically scholars have sought to understand and explain the ways policymakers remember the past. The normative claim is that institutional amnesia is a barrier to policy learning. That is, if the past is neglected then governments are destined to repeat failures (see Pollit 2008; King and Crewe 2013; Stark 2019; Stark and Head 2019). The decline thesis is therefore more than an intellectual enterprise; it seeks to instantiate change to the processes and practices of remembering in order to improve policymaking.

The scholar who has done the most to advance the recent discussion of institutional memory in government is Christopher Pollitt (2000, 2007, 2008, 2009). Pollitt cites a range of both endogenous and exogenous factors as contributing to the decline of institutional memory. He suggests that high rotation of staff, changes in IT systems which prevent proper archiving, regular organisational restructuring, rewarding management skills above all others, and adopting new management 'fads' as they become popular provide a perfect recipe for loss of institutional memory within organisations (Pollitt 2008: 173). According to Pollitt, the managerialist attitudes present in contemporary forms of government that favour constant change have encouraged the kind of 'contempt for the past' that underpins failures in record-keeping (Pollitt 2009: 207).

While Pollitt has been the most prolific contributor to academic arguments in favour of restoring institutional memory, he is not alone in lamenting its decline. Wettenhall (2011: 86) similarly identifies the new ways of doing government as enabling the factors that drive institutional memory loss, including cost-cutting drives, record-keeping functions developing a status as 'non-core' or unimportant, and frequent reorganising and changes to the workforce and downsizing. Using the case of Australia, Rhodes and Tiernan (2014: 214) suggest that geography has further compounded the problem of diminishing institutional memory, with the move to new Parliament House in 1988 isolating ministers and the prime minister from the public service.

How Is It Different to Policy Learning?

A problem with this conceptualisation of institutional memory is that it is hard to distinguish the concept from policy learning (Bennett and Howlett 1992: 288; for a fuller discussion see Dunlop and Radaelli 2013). Our first conceptual move is thus to differentiate between *learning* and *memory*. Bennett and Howlett (1992: 288) define policy learning very broadly as 'the general increase in knowledge about policies'. Based on this definition we could perhaps conceive of a continuum from learning to memory with an inflection point where one starts and the other stops. But this is easier to imagine than it is to measure empirically. It also doesn't acknowledge the forms memories take and the ways memories are contested, suppressed and actively forgotten, as well as the ways in which policy memories and ideas are transferred from elsewhere (Cairney 2009). Equally, there is no definitive point of disjunction between those components of learning and memory that are essentially documentary in nature and those that reside in the experience of individuals. Individuals build shared memories in which documents and their own experience combine to create a story of what happened. These stories are held at the level of organisations, and are given institutional form by the ways they help to shape future action as actors recall these past stories when faced with a new challenge. This helps to explain why the literature has not produced a definitive distinction between 'organisational memory' and 'institutional memory', with many authors using the terms almost interchangeably. For instance, Pollitt (2009: 202) often uses 'organisational memory', defined as 'consisting of a range of "storage" locations ... the experience and knowledge of the existing staff: what is "in their heads" ... the technical systems, including electronic databases and various kinds of paper records ... The management system ... and the norms and values of the organizational culture'.

The Role of Narrative

To resolve these conceptual shortcomings, we draw on the pioneering work of Linde and Czarniawska. Linde's (2009: 11) work on institutional memory and narrative foregrounds the role of interpretation by suggesting that memories are 'representations of the past'. As she puts it, '[i]nstitutions certainly make efforts to preserve aspects of their past, to find and retrieve some of these representations of the past, and to use them in the present to influence the future. Let us call it memory ' (Linde 2009: 11). She then differentiates the different 'modes of remembering' that are available. '[T]here exist a spectrum of modes of remembering within institutions. These range from strategies relying on individual human memory and transmissions from human to human, through archival and computer storage of documents ... to organisational policies and procedures and even physical infrastructure' (Linde 2009: 11).

Uniting Linde and Pollitt's approaches to institutional memory are two things. First, an emphasis on knowledge (and hence the close link to studies of policy learning). We can read Linde as viewing memory and learning as inextricably interrelated, operating as an iterative duality. We therefore define memories as the 'representations of the past' that actors draw on to *narrate* what has been learned when developing and implementing policy. When these narratives are embedded in *processes* they become 'institutionalised'. It is this emphasis on *embedded narratives* that distinguishes institutional memory from policy learning and its emphasis on increasing or improving knowledge about policy. Institutional memory may facilitate policy learning but equally, 'static' memories may prohibit genuine adaptation and innovation. As a result, while there is an obvious affinity between the two concepts it is imperative that they remain distinct avenues of enquiry. Policy learning has unequivocally positive connotations that are echoed in some conceptualisations of institutional memory (e.g. Pollitt). But, equally, memory (at least in a 'static' form) can be said to provide administrative agents with an advantage over political principals.

Second, this work draws attention to the different *forms* that institutional memory takes – residing within people, documents, policies and procedures and so on. Recognition of the different forms memories take highlights the significance of communication in the processes and practices of remembering. Here, we turn to Czarniawska's work on knowledge, narrative and organisational identity. Drawing on literary theory in particular, Czarniawska (1997: 6) shifts the emphasis from knowledge as something that is 'out there' waiting to be discovered to the forms in which knowledge is cast and the effects this has on institutions: 'The narrative mode of knowing consists in organizing experience with the help of a scheme assuming the intentionality of human action' (Czarniawska 2004: 18). The point, from our perspective, is that memory is more than a collection of facts and figures; it functions as a dramatised story (Boje 1991a, 1991b). It has a plot. It has characters. There are different genres. But all have a narrative arc that operates to sequence key events and decisions which then take shape as stories masquerading as memories. As Czarniawska puts it, '"The company suffered unprecedented losses" and "the general manager was forced to resign" are two events that call for interpretation ... the difference lies in the temporal ordering, and suggested connection between the two' (Czarniawska 1997: 14). In other words, 'some kind of causality may be inferred but it is crucial to see that narrative, unlike science, leaves open the nature of the connection' (Czarniawska 2004: 18).

In relation to our arguments here, the key point is that institutionalising memory – embedding representations of the past in processes – is not something that only occurs after a given policy decision is taken, or a policy implemented, but rather actors are continuously engaged in this dynamic practice. As Czarniawska (1997: 24) highlights, faced with the task of accounting for their actions, actors justify themselves by employing their knowledge of the institution and its past in narrative form to explain why they did what they did. Like Linde, Czarniawska argues that repertoires vary, but the goal – to create a narrative that is as coherent as possible – is similar to all individuals and the institutions they inhabit. Indeed, we might go as far as to claim that it is the appearance of a coherent narrative that constitutes the institution (Bevir and Rhodes 2010; Corbett and Howard 2017). Institutional memory is thus, for Czarniawska, a never-ending form of storytelling in which the key institutional questions are, who are we? what do we do? and how do we typically operate?

Are There 'Better' Memories and If So How Might They Be Captured?

Having established a working conception of institutional memory that emphasises its narrative, storytelling form, it is also necessary to examine its purpose – what is institutional memory for and what impact can it have on an organisation?

Walsh and Ungson (1991) distinguish between several different functions of institutional memory, including learning, impacts on organisational culture, and the entrenchment of existing power bases. Pollitt's thesis emphasises (and laments the decline of) the positive effect of memory on decision-making. Early literature on institutional memory described negative and positive effects of remembering the past. Those emphasising negative effects suggested that memories limit the range of solutions that an institution will consider (March 1972, 2010; Nystrom and Starbuck 1984). Authors emphasising positive effects suggested that memories of past events can result in improved decision-making through better anticipating causal associations (Duncan and Weiss 1979; Schon 1983). For the most part, however, these authors relied on a 'static' conceptualisation of institutional memory. We venture that a more 'dynamic' conceptualisation has the potential to mitigate some of the negatives and accentuate some of the advantages that these scholars identify.

How an institution might improve its memory is intrinsically linked to how memory is defined and whether or not it is in decline. If we follow Pollitt's view that memory is about the archive of accumulated knowledge that is being ignored or deliberately dismantled by managerialism, then the answer involves returning to an older way of doing government that placed a higher value on experience. By placing a higher value on the past as a resource, institutions would reduce staff turnover, and stop regular restructures, changes in IT systems and so on. For those of us who work in an institution where restructuring and IT changes are the norm, this solution has obvious attractions. But, would it improve memory? Or would it simply make it easier to preserve the status quo (a process that involves actively forgetting disruptive but generative innovations)?

By contrast, if institutional memory operates as a form of storytelling that links past policy lessons with present policy problems, it is reasonable to then ask whether it's possible to distinguish between 'true' and 'false' memories in a narrative mode of knowing. Again, we build on Czarniawska, who argues that in a narrative mode, the plausibility of the knowledge claim is determined by the plot. Thus, 'A narrative which says "The top managers resigned and then it rained a whole week" (i.e. a narrative with no plot or an incomprehensible plot) will need some additional elements to make sense of it, even though the two events and their temporal connection may well be true and correct in themselves' (Czarniawska 2004: 18). In which case, a narrative approach to knowledge and memory that emphasises its dynamic nature does not mean abandoning agreed facts or truths, but rather recognises that they cannot speak for themselves. In being spoken, however, they reveal a polyphony of interpretations, subplots and rival accounts. It is these rival accounts that illustrate the dynamic nature of institutional memory.

Our definition, relying as it does on a more dynamic conceptualisation of memory, is sceptical about the need to improve practices of remembering. But, if an institution did want to remember better we would favour increasing the opportunity for actors within an institution to reflect on and narrate the past. We return to this point in Section 6, where we explore a number of issues pertinent for organisations wishing to improve memory retention and use, as well as for scholars researching processes of governance that touch on institutional memory.

Towards a Dynamic View of Memories in Institutional Contexts

Existing work has highlighted the need for governments to rethink memory, not simply as a record of the past but as a vital tool for building the policy future. But, with the exception of Linde and Czarniawska, to date the proposed solutions to the perceived decline in institutional memory largely involve recourse to older ways of doing government. Even if returning to the past were desirable, we argue that it is no longer feasible because of the dispersed nature of contemporary governance (Hendriks 2009; Marsh 2011; Bouckaert 2017). Working across agency boundaries is now 'essential to the core business of government' (Carey and Crammond 2015:1020) and 'the new normal' (Sullivan 2015: 120–122). To build on Pollitt's work, we therefore argue that a dynamic conception of institutional memory must include knowledge that is both scattered between organisations and difficult to express. Ontologically, we follow Linde and Czarniawska in a shift away from the recording of objective 'facts' on a paper file, and towards an understanding of institutional memories as dynamic 'live conversations.' Epistemologically, this means a shift to allow for the construction and interpretation of multiple memories rather than one agreed memory such as that which might be rendered by a set of minutes. To capture this, we need to build a new way of conceptualising institutional memories from the ground up. These shifts are outlined in Table 1.

As we illustrate in our empirical discussion in the sections that follow, current practitioners provide evidence that supports Pollitt's contentions around a decline in institutional memory, but remain unsure about how the decline can be arrested. Stopping position churn, reinserting public servants into ministerial offices, reinvigorating better record management practices and other decisions would arguably still not enable governments to capture distributed memory. Instead, thinking of memories as 'living conversations' spread across a hybrid of actors offers opportunities for breaking down this kind of individualised atomisation of memory, and suggests new avenues for retaining it.

A dynamic conceptualisation thus emphasises how the past is communicated, rather than merely recorded, with the telling of stories playing a central role

Table 1 The Spectrum of Institutional Memories

'Static' Institutional Memory	'Dynamic' Institutional Memories
• Located in individual departments	• Whole-of-government memory processes
• Summative – end-of-project evaluation	• Formative – an iterative conversation
• Focused on the civil service	• Held in common across hybrids of actors
• Takes a material form: paper or digital files	• Is about people: stored as 'living' memory through a combination of fresh perspectives, individual agency and shared stories

(Czarniawska 1997; Linde 2009; Rhodes 2011; Stark 2019). For example, Linde argues that 'occasions' (such as staff functions, speeches, etc.) represent environments in which stories about an organisation's history, purpose and trajectory are rehearsed and internalised. They represent the moments when 'the process of institutional remembering can be deliberately altered' (Linde 2009: 222). She suggests that while an institution keeps existing, new stories will be added to the collection of disasters (what not to do), triumphs (what to do) and changes in direction, and new 'heroes' will emerge to act as role models for others to follow (Linde 2009: 222).

A more dispersed form of memory does not of course guarantee dynamism. It is theoretically possible for even a widely dispersed memory to remain trapped within locked documentary files, or indeed untold by individuals, and thus held mute in multiple places by dispersed actors. What causes static memory to become dynamic is constant retrieval and re-evaluation through social interaction between actors as they translate static documents into living memories. This reflects the nature of the spectrum outlined in Table 1 as being relatively fluid rather than a stark binary. For example, government reports frequently have a narrative grow around them that becomes embedded as part of the story. As we discuss in our case study on the roll-out of smart meters in Victoria, Australia (Section 3), key documents like the auditor-general's report remain an integral part of the memory of that policy implementation process and the 'story' of failure that is told about it, acting to reinforce the credibility of the story.

This emphasis on storytelling offers an inherently iterative conceptual key for unlocking a more dynamic form of institutional memory. It draws our attention to *actors* as the key disseminators and repositories of memory. A dynamic approach to institutional memories therefore conceptualises storytelling as a *social* phenomenon that can be exchanged both within and between organisations. It conceives of memories as the intersubjective retelling of events that imbues them with *meaning*. In which case, remembering is not so much about retrieving facts and files, but received traditions: ways of seeing the world and acting in it.

Method and Data

If memories are fundamentally about storytelling, and this way of thinking has empirical salience in highly networked and differentiated policy environments, then evaluating whether current practices and processes of remembering differ from the more static conceptualisation requires a particular approach to collecting and analysing data. In particular, the emphasis on storytelling invokes the main precepts of the discursive turn in the social and policy sciences (Fischer 2003; Schmidt 2008, 2010; Stone 2012). It also moves us away from more traditional variants of historical institutionalism towards more 'actor-centred' approaches (e.g. Bell 2011) and what Bevir and Rhodes (2010) term 'situated agency' (see Smullen 2010; Elston 2014; Corbett and Howard 2017). The point of this distinction is that by recognising the plurality of actors and their memories, the latter approach offers a more dynamic rendering than the former static view.

Many of Pollitt's (2008) empirical observations on institutional memory are based on British, Australian and New Zealand cases. Following Pollitt, we draw our case studies from the same jurisdictions, both to hold the Westminster system of government constant (see Rhodes, Wanna and Weller 2009), and to test whether a more dynamic version of institutional memory could mitigate against the declines that Pollitt finds in those jurisdictions. Our aim in presenting these case studies – explored in Sections 2 to 5 – is to illustrate, rather than 'prove', that our conceptualisation has empirical purchase (Boswell, Corbett and Rhodes 2019). That is, we aim, building on the work of others, to reorient the field, and so this Element is designed as the first stone rather than the last word.

In each of our four sections our empirical material is similar: for each we drew on a combination of in-depth interviews with key actors and the public record to both reconstruct the process by which the policy in question was made, and probe how memory was captured in each instance. The interviewees in each case study were deliberately chosen in order to ensure both a vertical and horizontal spread. Vertically, we set out to capture the insights of heads of agency *and* the mid-level civil servants undertaking the substantive policy

Table 2 Dataset

Case Study	Dataset	National or Subnational	Collaboration across Government, or between Government and External Actors
Family Violence Action Plan, Tasmania (Australia)	9 interviews and public documents	Subnational	Across government
Smart Meters Victoria (Australia)	11 interviews and public documents	Subnational	Government and external actors
Zero Carbon Homes, United Kingdom	10 interviews, public documents, memoirs	National	Government and external actors
The justice sector, New Zealand	10 interviews and public documents	National	Across government

work. Horizontally, in the two case studies representing hybrid collaborations – in Victoria, Australia and the United Kingdom – we interviewed not just government actors, but also representatives from collaborating organisations to see whether their 'memories' of a particular policy process matched or not, and to compare policy learning. Table 2 summarises our approach.

Key Findings

Table 3 captures the ways in which memories were meaningfully operational-ised to prevent memory loss across our four policy case studies. These four dynamic forms of institutional memory are explored across Sections 2 to 5, with each section discussing one type of dynamic memory.

The empirical analysis in the sections that follow illustrates how narratives become embedded in institutional processes and practices, with actors combining documentary records and files with their own memories of what happened. What emerges over time are collective stories that frame past events as a success or failure. But, while their embedded nature implies path dependence, we caution that they nevertheless remain open to change as actors reinterpret the degree of success or failure in light of new information and events. It is this ability to recast memories that renders them dynamic.

Table 3 Embedding Dynamic, Actor-Centred Memories In Institutional
Processes

'Dynamic' Institutional Memories	Operationalised	Illustrative Case Study
Collaborative, whole-of-government memory processes	Policy processes contain a mixture of 'old hands' and newer talent, drawn from across government, allowing memories to be dispersed in an iterative process	Section 2: Family Violence Action Plan, Tasmania (Australia)
Formative – an iterative conversation	Forum 'occasions' become institutionalised and augmented to ensure that a plurality of voices is heard	Section 3: Smart Meters, Victoria (Australia)
Held in common across hybrids of actors	Physically locate people together in 'hubs', 'task forces' or 'steering groups' for portions of the policy process	Section 4: Zero Carbon Homes, United Kingdom
Stored as 'living' memories through a combination of fresh perspectives, individual agency and shared stories	A core rhetorical device that represents shared understandings, and reminds participants about key elements of networked memory	Section 5: The Justice Sector, New Zealand

The four sections provide insights into the myriad ways in which institutional memories are created and retold. Interview responses show a spectrum of practice, with various degrees of reliance on a mixture of informal storytelling and formal documentation that emerges from the more traditional types of departmental processes. We are not suggesting that these mechanisms are exhaustive or will work the same way in every policy setting. Nor are we suggesting that bureaucracies can or should simply give up formalised ways of remembering through files, minutes and other memory aids. Documentary memories remain necessary for modern institutions; our argument is simply that they are not sufficient in themselves as a way of storing memory. While they remain vital, they do not exist as some objective form of knowledge waiting to be retrieved by actors. Rather, the research presented here suggests that actors are using socially constructed forms of memory in tandem with existing static memory structures and procedures. While this is not a new occurrence, we suggest that with increasing collaborative governance it has become more central. Moreover, it is evolving a form of practice that has left current static theories of institutional memory in its wake.

Structure of the Element

With this introductory section having set out the case for studying institutional memory within government, and our ideas about a more dynamic conceptualisation of memory, the majority of the remainder of the Element focuses on our four empirical case studies, with each case study comprising a section.

Section 2 is about the role of memory in the development of the Family Violence Action Plan in the state of Tasmania, Australia. In 2015, Rosie Batty was made Australian of the Year for her outspoken advocacy on behalf of the victims of domestic violence. Her leadership galvanised a national conversation, and in August 2015 the Tasmanian government pledged over AU$25 million for a new statewide action plan to tackle family violence. The release of the plan was the culmination of a rapid eight-week policy development process, undertaken after state government departments and external stakeholders had set up bespoke institutional structures to deliver the plan. This included a dedicated cabinet subcommittee, a committee of the heads of the relevant agencies who met weekly throughout the process, and a working group from across government that were physically located together for two days a week while they worked on the plan. This kind of collaboration within government was further supported by an external consultative group, built from existing connections. In Section 2 we examine how and why institutional memory contributed to the success of the action plan, with a focus on whole-of-government processes and the creation of collective memories.

Section 3 is also an Australian case study, concentrating on the mandatory installation of 'smart meters' in the state of Victoria. However, unlike the Family Violence Action Plan detailed in Section 2, this policy was less successful. The Advanced Metering Infrastructure (AMI) programme in Victoria was agreed upon in 2006, and implemented in the period 2009–2013. The AMI programme involved the mandatory installation of so-called 'smart meters' – communications-enabled digital electricity meters – in every household and business in Victoria. It was subject to widespread criticism: there were large increases in customer bills, escalating installation costs, and a range of technical problems. The private sector played an integral role in the AMI programme delivery. Utility distribution companies were the main type of organisation contracted to implement the AMI programme, with the state government providing oversight. Crucially, it was the nature of this relationship – and the lack of public sector leadership – that was criticised heavily by the Victorian Auditor-General, who was called in to review the AMI in 2009, and again in 2015. The institutional memories held about the project centre around this negative perception. Other Australian states examining options for introducing smart meters have consciously used the Victorian experience as a model of what *not* to do. Section 3 focuses on the role of iterative conversations in forming dynamic memories.

Section 4 is about the Zero Carbon Homes policy in the UK, and considers the role in memory formation and retention of collaborative 'hubs' or forums where key decision makers actively collaborate. In December 2006 the UK Labour government published a consultation document setting out plans to move towards zero carbon in new housing by 2016. The policy continued under the coalition government in 2010 but it was amended to balance the zero carbon target with the stimulation of growth in the housebuilding industry. The concept of 'Allowable Solutions' was thus introduced to include off-site carbon reductions. After nine years, and one year before it was scheduled to come into effect, the Conservative government announced that it no longer intended to proceed with the policy, citing its aim to reduce net regulation and stimulate housebuilding activities. The policy is of interest in relation to institutional memory for two reasons. First, it involved several years of intense collaboration between different public and private stake-holders facilitated by a public–private organisation – the Zero Carbon Hub – allowing us to investigate the construction of memory among hybrids of actors. Second, these deliberations were underpinned by considerable research into and development into the technical dimensions of the policy. This technical knowledge has considerable value beyond simple lessons learned, and forms a central part of what actors now 'remember' of the process.

Section 5 focuses on the formation of the 'justice sector' in New Zealand. From 2008, five New Zealand agencies – the Ministry of Justice, the New Zealand Police, the Department of Corrections, the Crown Law Office and the Serious Fraud Office – became collectively known as the Justice Sector. This collection of agencies has worked collaboratively by setting strategy, pooling funding to seed new innovations, and coordinating delivery. Collectively the five agencies employ 23,000 people and are responsible for several billion dollars of expenditure. The justice sector comprises agencies with regimented, hierarchical cultures. Their method of collaboration reflects this: monthly meetings of agency chief executives, fortnightly meetings of deputy-chief executives, formal terms of reference, papers, motions, minutes, etc. The justice sector is considered by public servants to be one of the most effective attempts at cross-agency collaboration in New Zealand (see, for example, Scott and Boyd 2017, 2020). The way it captures and communicates information provides important insights into how actors can create memories across departments without being restrained by traditional siloes. Section 5 examines the ways in which the New Zealand justice sector has fostered the creation of 'living' memories.

Section 6 concludes the Element by summarising our findings and suggesting a number of ways forward in terms of research and also for practitioners. This Element represents one set of arguments about how the scholarship on institutional memory might be able to further flourish and expand. The increasingly networked context in which policy is currently being made, defined as it is by increased speed and collaboration, requires a more consciously dynamic conceptualisation of institutional memory that both better captures how the past is currently being recorded in different governing contexts, and provides an opportunity to think through how these practices might be strengthened. Rather than a return to a past way of operating, a dynamic actor-centred conceptualisation offers a way of reinterpreting past traditions *into* the present. In doing so we shift the scholarly focus: from institutional *memory* to institutional *memories*.

2 Whole-of-Government Processes and the Creation of Collective Memories: The Case of the Tasmanian Family Violence Action Plan

'Dynamic' Institutional Memories	Operationalised	Illustrative Case Study
Whole-of-government memory processes	Policy processes contain a mixture of 'old hands' and newer talent, drawn from across government, allowing memories to be dispersed in an iterative process	Family Violence Action Plan, Tasmania (Australia)

Policies rarely emerge in a vacuum. That may indeed be the only point of agreement in the literature between the many contending theoretical conceptualisations of the policy process (see Peters 2015 for a good overview). How an idea emerges matters not just for how the policy process then takes shape, but also how that process is subsequently remembered by the institutions who conducted it. The shaping of family violence policy in the Australian state of Tasmania in 2015 is a case in point. The policy emerged amidst an intense national focus on the issue, driven in part by a policy entrepreneur, in ways commensurate with Kingdon's (1984) well-known 'multiple streams' theory. But as will become clear later in this section, the kind of fast-paced policy process that might suit a 'policy window' of this kind can lead to a form of institutional memory that creates unrealistic expectations of replicability.

Kingdon's 'multiple streams' approach posits that three streams coexist within the policy ether at any given point in time: a problem stream, a policy stream and a politics stream. At the point of fluvial convergence when these three streams come together, a 'policy window' opens, providing an opportunity for an issue to emerge. What allows that issue to gain prominence and traction is the role played by a 'policy entrepreneur' in pushing forward while the three streams are aligned. This is exactly the scenario that played out in Australia – and in the state of Tasmania specifically – around the issue of family violence, with the role of policy entrepreneur filled by the 2015 Australian of the Year, Rosie Batty (see Hawley, Clifford and Konkes 2018).

Rosie Batty's heart-rending personal story and first-hand experience of the horrors of extreme family violence drove her to start a campaign that very quickly made her a public figure. In February 2014, her eleven-year-old son was murdered by his father, Greg Anderson, at a suburban oval in Melbourne during cricket practice. Batty herself had experienced years of physical abuse at Anderson's hands. The media interest in the case was high, and Batty immediately made the decision to speak out about her experience. As she stated when accepting her Australian of the Year award and dedicating it to her son Luke, 'He is the reason I have found my voice and I'm able to be heard.' She founded the Luke Batty Foundation in 2014 to advocate for change – both culturally and legally – in the way that the Australian community responds to family violence.

At both a national and subnational level, governments across Australia injected new urgency into policy proposals to change the conversation around family violence while putting in place greater protection and support for sufferers. Under the leadership of Premier Will Hodgman, the Tasmanian State Government was an early mover. From the start, the Tasmanian policy response was billed as being a 'whole-of-government' process. The literature in public administration has for nearly two decades now analysed and promoted 'joined-up government' and whole-of-government approaches as the way to break down the siloes that hold back effective policymaking (see Christensen and Lægreid 2007). It has particularly been seen as a way of dealing with social problems that can be characterised as 'wicked problems' (Rittel and Webber 1973; Head and Alford 2015). Issues of domestic violence display many of the characteristics of wicked problems, in particular the incapacity to easily identify the specific causal variables that could be targeted by government policy.

While there are few actual critiques of the idea of 'joined-up government' or 'whole-of-government' approaches, there are manifold examples of just how difficult they are to achieve in practice. One under-theorised aspect of whole-of-government operations is how they can effectively draw on institutional memory when it so often resides in individual departments. Just as importantly, there is little empirical evidence on how whole-of-government initiatives capture shared memories themselves so that they can be passed on for future operations. These problems will be examined later in this section in trying to analytically grapple with the lessons to be drawn from the Tasmanian case study.

One of the notable successes of how the Tasmanian government set out to tackle family violence was in the clarity of not just the message but the institutional support provided to turn it into reality. The government very consciously set in place three component parts that would ensure that the policy formulation process would go on to be considered a success in whole-of-government policymaking. First, it ensured there was political buy-in at the highest level. Not only was the Premier taking a personal interest in the policy, a cabinet committee was also set up to oversee the formulation process. The government also took care to reach out early to opposition parties to try and find some cross-party consensus to make sure domestic violence would not become a party-political battleground.

Second, they put in place bureaucratic structures that cut across traditional governmental siloes. A secretaries group, comprising the heads of all the relevant line departments and the head of the Department of Premier and Cabinet (DPAC), met weekly to oversee the work. This direct alignment between political and bureaucratic leadership prevented any sense of operational slippage due to a lack of vigilance.

Third, this joined-up leadership model was replicated in the team of public servants charged with creating and shaping the policy framework. Public servants from all the relevant agencies – police, justice, DPAC, and more – were joined together in a delivery task force. Crucially, this was not the usual cross-departmental working group that would get together for regular meetings but split apart to do the work. This group was in fact physically brought together by being co-located for two days a week. As ideas and difficulties emerged a quick conversation with others in the room was able to fix a snag that might have, in the normal course of events, simply been held over until the next task force meeting.

The structure of what follows in this section draws out these three components that were successfully held in alignment. The analysis then connects these three aspects more explicitly to questions of institutional memory. We discuss how much impact institutional memory had on the development of the policy, and the expectations of the actors involved about how the process will itself now be remembered in the future. One recurring theme will be the relative advantages to be gained from operating within a small jurisdiction, in which established relationships allowed for relative speed and flexibility of movement based on previous connections. Similarly, interview data suggest that the largely positive perceptions of the policy process have led to an embedded narrative of success – which has the paradoxical capacity to limit potential future innovation.

The Start: Political Drive

There is now an extensive literature on the role of democratic leaders in shaping policy priorities for their governments (Kane and Patapan 2012; 't Hart 2014; Bennister, Worthy and 't Hart 2017). What leaders choose to focus on matters because it sucks away oxygen from other policy areas. The flip side, of course, is that it also means that the areas of focus that are chosen are imbued with a real sense of political drive. That was certainly the case with the issue of family violence in Tasmania. In late May 2015, the Tasmanian Premier Will Hodgman briefed that this policy area would be a major focus for his government going forward. He emphasised that he himself would lead that push. This was set out first in a speech he gave to a White Ribbon function in Hobart on 25 May 2015. This had been trailed in the media ahead of time, with the main local newspaper – the *Mercury* – publishing a supportive piece outlining the government's planned focus (Hope 2015).

The proposed plan itself was brought into sharper relief on 2 June 2015, with the government issuing a press release setting out its policy approach on family violence. Crucially, the announcement was accompanied by an unusual degree of specificity on what was happening and how long things would take. The announcement committed the government to releasing the plan in August. It also revealed that a special subcommittee of cabinet had been set up to drive the agenda, that an external consultative group would be established within the first week, and that the plan would be a demonstrably 'whole-of-government' response.

It is of course nothing new for governments to make big announcements and trumpet strong commitments. But the embedding of these goals within bespoke institutional architectures is less usual, and was certainly noticed by the public servants who would be tasked with the nuts and bolts of the work. Many of those we interviewed were struck by the impact that had:

> The project, or the plan, the commitment was born from the leadership of the Premier, the leadership of his ministers, and the leadership of the Secretary of the Department who was deeply committed to the development of the plan and to action. They at various times early on in the piece came along and spoke to the task force, and that was really powerful because it gave us a licence to think big and to think outside the box and to convey their commitment at a deep and serious level to be addressing this issue. (Interview)

This was also the result of a very overt attempt at a political level to depoliticise the issue to create the space for political cohesion. As recalled by one of the responsible ministers, there was a conscious sense of buy-in across the political spectrum, with a group of strong women politicians playing prominent roles. 'I said if there's one issue that we can truly make above politics, can we please make it family violence and tackle it together. So together, we organised for the first debate in Parliament that really had tripartisan support' (interview).

Establishing Whole-of-Government Processes

Political drive is essential to successful policymaking. But in social science terms it is a 'necessary but not sufficient' condition for action. In this case, the politics was underpinned by processes that were explicitly whole-of-government in ways that are empirically examinable. First, as suggested above, the cabinet subcommittee was mirrored by a committee of departmental secretaries beneath it, drawn in from all the relevant departments. To give that process urgency, the committee met on a weekly basis, with further dynamic communication patterns outside of the meetings themselves. This is one example of where jurisdictional size made a difference, as noted by one departmental head:

> I've always believed in Tasmania that, within the public sector and indeed within Tasmanian life more broadly, leadership is exercised through relationships in networks. It's what makes this state function. It's one of the beauties of having a relatively small system – everybody knows each other and, when the relationships are strong, you can take action quickly and collaboratively . . . So when we need to take collective action, we don't send each other letters and wait for a response, we get on the phone. We see each other in the street. (Interview)

This degree of senior buy-in was mirrored outside the government itself through the external consultative group that was set up right at the beginning of the process. This is another example of where small jurisdictional size seems to have had an impact. In larger jurisdictions, the idea that you could get all key stakeholders around a table, bringing with them policy suggestions as well as analytical insight, in order to arrive at an action plan in a period of weeks would be considered laughably ambitious. Several aspects made it possible here. First, the relatively small size of Tasmanian civil society meant that the actors already knew each other well and were used to working together. Second, there were already existing group structures in place for dealing with aspects of domestic violence; so while the focus and the particular piece of policy may have been new, the surrounding policy infrastructure was not.

The make-up of the external consultative group, as confirmed by media release on 17 June (Hodgman 2015), was wide-ranging. It included organisations used to supporting the victims of domestic violence, such as women's shelters and sexual assault support services, but then also included representatives from different sectors of society, including Aboriginal organisations, the Farmers and Graziers Association, the migrant resource centre and disability support organisations. In short, the goal of establishing a 'whole-of-government' response was reflected in the make-up of an equally broad external consultative group that might deliver a wider degree of community engagement.

Having thus established a level of community buy-in to match the political and bureaucratic commitment, what drove the project forward was the bringing together of a cross-departmental working group of public servants. As discussed, the fact that this group was physically co-located together for two days each week was a specific innovation. It was a physical expression that backed up the intention that those working on the action plan should make it their highest priority.

For most of the participants, this co-location was a key part of what drove the policy process forward. From an institutional memory point of view, one of the insights here is that members of the co-located task force acted as conduits back to their home departments. In other words, they developed the narrative of the policy process and shared it iteratively as they went along: '[W]e spent some time sharing information on how we wanted to work and one of the aspects was that we recognised that we were conduits back to our own agencies and that we would bring to the task force the collective views of our officers in agencies' (interview).

In line with the theme of this section, one of the key aspects in setting up the co-located task force was to ensure that there was a mixture of officers assigned to it, some who came with institutional memory and some who came with little. It appears that this combination worked well in two directions. First, it meant there was sufficient experience in policy processes to know how to make things work effectively. Second, it meant there was enough 'new blood' to avoid the kind of innovation-stifling path dependency that might otherwise have set in. One interviewee described it this way:

I guess that's the benefit of having a mixture of people in organisations, some of which are new and fresh, and there's a real benefit to having a fresh set of eyes and not being drawn down by the past, and a combination of people who've been doing things for a long time and have that experience. The old hands. So I guess a combination of both is not necessarily a bad thing. (Interview)

Memories

The public servants in the task force drew at the outset on whatever institutional memory was available on how 'whole-of-government' initiatives had previously been made to work at a process level. For example, one described a previous whole-of-government group that had been called together to address a bush fire crisis:

I did call someone who'd been involved in the bush fire task force early on just to – it was a very quick phone call but it was, 'What are the lessons? What worked well when you pulled together for a short period of time, a team from across Government to address the bush fires? What was important in terms of getting that task force or that group of people working well together?' And the two pieces of information he reflected on were the importance of leadership and the importance of communication. (Interview)

The issue with these institutional memories was that they were neither systematically stored nor systematically used. As another public servant reflected, the lessons from that bush fire response were not always fully utilised when putting together the Family Violence Action Plan: 'The bush fire task force was one that was a whole of government [initiative]. It was a very quick crisis response, so it got people together. It had cultural differences. How do people work through the cultural differences from different agencies? All sorts of amazing little tools and techniques, but did we use it? No' (interview).

As part of this case study, all participants were asked how they felt the policy process would be remembered, and whether it was something they thought governments would ask them to replicate in the future. Their responses speak to the positives of a more dynamic, iteratively spread conceptualisation of institutional memory, but also highlight its limitations in combating the presentism bias that has always complicated memory processes. The responses can be broken into three distinct categories: those who felt that lessons would be quickly forgotten; those who felt that lessons would be remembered but only within a narrow band of policy challenges that would suit this style of process; and those who saw genuine longer-term memories becoming embedded as narratives of how policy can be made.

Those at the pessimistic end felt that governments perform poorly at retaining memories because there is no incentive and little commitment to actually institutionalise memories. What's more, the very act of institutionalisation itself may lock in a newly path-dependent way of doing things that prevents the kind of nimbleness that guaranteed the success in the first place:

> Well of course we'd want to capture the good learnings from this type of process but I have to say I don't think in my experience in government we've ever been very good at that, and it's always a balance too, because you don't want to fall into the trap of saying, well, I remember ten years ago we tried this and it didn't work then and it isn't going to work now . . . So whilst I think there's a lot of room for us to be a lot better in terms of our institutional memory . . . it's also useful to have fresh sets of eyes on issues and problems. (Interview)

Multiple interviewees pointed to the need for a mix of memory and flexibility as being the most useful way to hold memory without being weighed down by it:

> It's also important in any project or policy or change management environment to make sure you've got some learnings, you're writing them down for history's sake as well so you don't, as you said before, make the mistakes of the past. But don't be so rigid that you've got a process that you need to follow and say, well, this point A is here, point B, sometimes it might be point A1, point A2, point A3 before you go to B, so you've got to adapt it for your own community, organisation and across the broader state. (Interview)

One interviewee joined the project towards the end of the planning process to help drive forward the actual implementation stage of the Family Violence Action Plan, and recalled how they felt they were able to pick up the lie of the land by connecting into the knowledge that had been 'owned' by the original task force group:

> It was a new area of focus for me in terms of my work, so I didn't come with a lot of content knowledge. But I think the main thing was that they had been a group that largely continued from the development phase into implementation and through that development phase they'd gone through a lot of activity, they'd formed strong relationships . . . Virtually six months in, I'm still cognisant of others being the holders of that information, particularly of things that happened at that time and needing to find that out. But [I'm] also [aware] – having been around the traps with the group for about six months now – of having absorbed some of that [information] as well and feeling a bit more comfortable in that space. (Interview)

When pressed about how that knowledge was retained and passed on, the interviewee nominated the combination of 'person-to-person' transfer with good documentation in terms of meetings, processes and outcomes. This allowed them to be able to pair their reading of a document with the first-hand information of those who had been involved in the actual event that was being documented. In some ways, it operates almost as a form of triangulation; the 'objective' data is supplemented by the 'subjective' voices of those who were there, to create an overall narrative that then gets retained as memory.

Another interviewee stressed the same point that the combination of personal memory and documentary support was powerful in memory terms:

> I think some of the knowledge sits with the individuals. However, enough individuals were involved in the process for there to be a collective memory and what I see now as we implement the action plan, we've got a consistency of involvement still from the agencies and we've got a level of trust that enables us to roll this out in a way that I feel is really efficient and really productive. But I also think it's really important that we document and, to some extent, we've done that. Shortly after the release of the policy, we undertook a review, a set of questions, with a range of people from the political offices through to the steering committee through to the task force members, and we've started – we've got a bit of a checklist. (Interview)

Finding ways to effectively operationalise memories relies on individuals feeling connected to the creation of those memories. As one interviewee reflected, '[I]n my own experience, unless you've lived it and breathed it yourself, you might own it at a conceptual level, but you don't necessarily own it at an emotional and behavioural level' (interview). The secret, according to this participant, is to make collaborative, cross-departmental ways of working the norm, rather than the exception, which leads naturally to a greater sharing of both knowledge and expertise. This is then evidenced in other policy areas, such as the writing of overarching briefs on government policy, for instance. 'We don't write briefs for health about health issues. We don't write briefs for education about education issues. We bring health here, we bring education here and we collectively write the brief ... That's happened over time and it's happened because leaders throughout the public service have modelled it' (interview).

Part of the rationale for supporting and maintaining institutional memory is that it allows a degree of learning from failure and possible replication of success. But even in a policy process widely held to be a success, many interviewees saw warning flags in terms of its potential replicability in other circumstances:

> There's a risk if it was replicated for all situations because the time frames meant that it was really guided towards and/or leant towards pacesetting, directive style leadership and action ... There were decisions that needed to be made where it wasn't possible, or appropriate even in some instances, to consult with all those involved, so that isn't something that you'd want to do all the time because it will put people offside. Also, the amount of energy for people as well ... it's probably the most exhausted I've seen people, to be blunt. (Interview)

A similar sentiment was confirmed by another interviewee, reflecting that the work had essentially been driven by the time frame in a way that wouldn't always be sustainable:

> Yes. I think the time frame drove it, essentially. And I think there are very good reasons why you'd take a bit longer in normal day-to-day government business to achieve things and to deliver things … and it relates to the complexity of the issues that we're working on, the need for engaging with the community and achieving buy-in … So all of that usually does take time and we did manage to achieve it in the short period of time, but probably not without cost as well. I think the pace that we were working isn't something that you'd sustain over a long period of time. (Interview)

It is perhaps understandable that from a political point of view in particular, this process would generate a desire to be able to repeat and replicate at will. The public servants involved were certainly not against that, but there was a wariness that this success should not translate into some kind of repetitive template. It is not a recipe that guarantees the same outcome from similar ingredients every time: '[W]e get questions like, "We should do this again. Let's do one of those. Let's do a family violence policy development," and it's not necessarily something that you can do every day and would want to do every day' (interview).

The Collective Shaping of Memory

If, as we contend throughout much of this Element, memories are held individually by actors who share them through narrative forms of storytelling, then can whole-of-government processes ever hope to be remembered effectively? Governments themselves remain set up as collections of individual departments. Even in small jurisdictions like Tasmania, there seems little alternative to traditional departmental structures. It's how Westminster systems of government work. This simple reality suggests that whole-of-government policy processes are likely to remain the exception rather than the norm; collections of actors brought together for a particular policy purpose and then being disbanded when the job is done.

What the Tasmanian case study suggests is that there is some reason for optimism that memories from whole-of-government processes can be not only retained but repurposed to new scenarios under the right conditions. To begin with, the very nature of whole-of-government activities means that they are likely to be organised by a central agency. In the Tasmanian case, that role was played by the Department of Premier and Cabinet. They hosted the task force of co-located public servants from other departments. DPAC is therefore also the natural host for the file-based evidence that seeks to document the process followed in ways synonymous with what we would traditionally think of as institutional memory. In other words, actors in the future who are looking for files on the Tasmanian Family Violence Action Plan have somewhere central to go.

As several of the public servants discussed in their interviews, this kind of documentation is important; it is necessary for effective institutional memory. But crucially for our arguments here, it is mixed with the more subjective experiences of individual actors that they retain themselves but build and share through interactions. The story grows in the telling as they return to their own departments and instinctively seek to apply some of the lessons learned to new policy areas. This is very different to relying on some kind of documentary template. It is more likely to manifest through conversations led by people who were there. Let us imagine a hypothetical example in which the Department of Justice is asked to shape new policy on how to manage prison rehabilitation systems. The lead public servant, having served on the previous task force, might say, 'using a group of existing external stakeholders worked well on the Family Violence Action Plan; we should do the same thing here . . . ' An officer from the department might then ring up the policy team in DPAC and ask them how they went about setting up the stakeholder group, and whether there is any particularly useful documentation.

This is the kind of interaction that happens instinctively between individuals. The distribution of memories as conversations enables them to become institutionalised in the collective memories of people who continue to draw on them. That combines with the documentary record to create a living memory capable of being passed on through position churn, rather than being crushed by it. The mix of old hands and new in each policy process ensures that the memory does not get lost through natural attrition, either; when a leader retires or leaves the service, their memories remain in circulation.

But significant limitations remain. First, it is clear that institutional memory alone has little capacity to generate either political consensus or political will. The success of the Tasmanian action plan process was at least partly based on the degree of uniformity in political views, and the focused clarity of purpose from the Premier himself. Self-evidently, that level of political buy-in is not always available. So even if the institutional memory suggests that a particular approach will work, the political conditions may mitigate against it.

Second, size of jurisdiction is undoubtedly an intervening variable that shapes the way conversations within government take place (Corbett and Howard 2017). Replicating this kind of conversation-led model of memory becomes a different prospect in a large national jurisdiction, where the sheer number of people involved and the size of departments could potentially overwhelm memories rather than institutionalise them (Corbett, Veenendaal and Connell 2020). There is therefore the potential that the plurality of policy myths works against their institutionalisation. Most large countries are of course divided into subnational jurisdictions or devolved authorities which can more closely hope to mirror the Tasmanian experience. More research in both larger and smaller jurisdictions will help to identify and isolate these effects and what they mean for institutional memory.

Third, it's possible for memories to become straitjackets of expectation that stifle innovation and fresh thinking. Path dependency in policymaking is a very real constraint. Many interviewees were aware of that possibility and stressed the need to avoid over-institutionalising practices that might only have been success-ful because of the confines of the specific policy context. Each policy challenge remains essentially unique. That is the signature observation to be drawn from the theoretical insights of both Kingdon's multiple streams theory and Rittel and Webber's wicked problems conceptualisation. Policy windows open and close at unpredictable times. Policy entrepreneurs can labour for years without reward only to find themselves suddenly thrust into the limelight at a key moment. Conceptualising whole-of-government memories as dynamic conversations allows for the creative reapplication of past success in reshaped ways to unique new circumstances.

3 What Happens with Iterative Conversations in Cases of Policy Failure: The State of Victoria's Smart Metering Programme, Australia

'Dynamic' Institutional Memories	Operationalised	Illustrative Case Study
Formative – an iterative conversation	Forum 'occasions' become institutionalised and augmented to ensure that a plurality of voices is heard	Smart meters, Victoria (Australia)

The focus of this section is on the dynamic conversations that comprise mem-ory, across a plurality of actors. It contrasts the iterative and flexible nature of conversations (a key aspect of dynamic memory) with more formal record-keeping practised by governments (static memory). These issues are explored using a case of the mandatory smart or 'advanced' metering infrastructure

(AMI) programme in Victoria, Australia, which ran from 2009 to 2013. The AMI programme encountered numerous difficulties, from cost overruns to failure in communication networks, leading to negative media attention and public protests, such that it came to be widely recognised as a policy failure. The section draws on empirical data comprising eleven interviews with public and private sector actors involved in the AMI programme, in the period April 2015 to November 2016.

We examine how the framing of the AMI programme as a policy failure limited the plurality of voices that were able to be heard, hence affecting what memories of the policy were formed. We show how there was an overwhelmingly dominant narrative about failure, which effectively silenced other voices, and dissuaded iterative conversations. There were not forum occasions in which a plurality of voices were able to be heard, quite simply because there was a strategic interest among key stakeholders in forgetting rather than remembering the smart metering policy. We show how policy failures create strong narratives, as opposed to iterative (flexible, dynamic) conversations, and that this results in selective amnesia – rather than memory building – with aspects of the policy actively forgotten. Institutional amnesia, the counterpart of institutional memory, is defined as '*the declining ability – and willingness – of public sector institutions in many countries to access and make use of possibly relevant past experiences.*'(Pollitt 2000: 6, emphasis in original).

This section thus explores a contrasting case to our other three case studies, because of the narrative of policy failure and evidence of strategic or deliberate processes to encourage amnesia, rather than build memory.

As in the other three empirical sections in the Element, we ask of the Victorian smart metering policy, first, how it was built on past ways of knowing, and, second, how it is represented now, including the methods by which representations of the past have been embedded (or not) within institutionalised processes. In conclusion we advocate for multidimensional, contested, messy, contingent narratives that pay close attention to both successes and failures.

Changing Forms of Memory and Their Relationship to Policy Failure

Static memory is singular and held in document form, such as files and procedures. Dynamic memories reside with people and are thus dispersed across the array of actors that make up a differentiated polity (see Section 1). A more dynamic people-centred conceptualisation sees institutional memory as a composite of intersubjective memories open to change, with memories as representations of the past that actors draw on to narrate policy lessons. In dynamic forms of memory, the role of narratives is central. Policy actors (whether private or public sector) continually create stories about the past (Czarniawska 1997, 2004; Linde 2009). The coherence of the narrative is important: unless it is coherent it will not have traction and will fade from memory, or else fracture into multiple conflicting memories across a network.

However, there are dangers in viewing dynamic memories as positive. There are problems with dynamic forms of institutional memory, especially in relation to policy failures. There are useful insights from psychology here which clearly differentiate between positive and negative information; for example, one study reveals how negative information is given higher priority within organisations (Peeters and Czapinski 1990), another how the sharing of negative information creates closeness between individuals much more so than positive information (Bosson et al. 2006).

Such findings sit alongside a growing literature in political science on policy failures (see Dunlop 2017), including useful categorisation of types of failure, such as programme, process and political failures (McConnell 2010; Bovens and 't Hart 1996). Yet the connections between policy failure and institutional memory and amnesia could be more fully conceptualised. We suggest that in cases of policy failure the successes within such policies are more likely to be forgotten, because the policy narrative only functions well if it is coherent and dramatised, i.e. if the successes are left out (Lovell 2017). Thus a clear downside of dynamic forms of institutional memory, centred as they are on people-to-people conversations and storytelling, is that they act to facilitate institutional amnesia. The jury is still out on whether institutional amnesia is a good or a bad thing (Stark 2019; Stark and Head 2019), but with regard to policy learning it is relatively clear that institutional amnesia about policy failures acts to hinder learning.

The memory losses associated with dynamic forms of memory are compounded by another set of processes leading to institutional amnesia in cases of policy failure on the static side of memory, namely that processes of recording keeping are incomplete, i.e. they might not always include the full summary of the policy in all its detail (positive and negative), because of concerns about accountability, transparency and the possibility of access to these policy archives through freedom of information requests.

These issues are explored below using our empirical case, suggesting (1) that more dynamic forms of memory such as narratives make policy failures harder to forget, and (2) that systematic learning is hampered by these narratives as many things are left out of them, compounded by partial 'static' record-keeping within government.

The Advanced Metering Infrastructure (AMI) Programme

The Advanced Metering Infrastructure (AMI) programme in Victoria was agreed upon in 2006 and implemented in the period 2009–2013. The AMI programme involved the mandatory installation of so-called 'smart meters' – communications-enabled digital electricity meters – in every household and business in Victoria. Utility distribution companies were the main type of organisation contracted to implement the AMI programme, with the state government providing oversight: it was a collaborative public–private sector policy programme, with the state government taking a relatively 'hands off' role. In the period 2009 to 2013 2.8 million advanced meters were installed in 93 per cent of homes and small businesses across Victoria (Victorian Auditor-General's Office (VAGO) 2015). The installation process involved removing the old mechanical meter in each property and replacing it with a digital advanced meter. Customers were charged directly for the new meters, with Victorian households paying on average AU$760 extra on their bills in the period 2010–2015 because of additional metering charges (VAGO 2015: 29). The metering bill payment was a flat charge, not adjusted according to house-hold income. It was anticipated that customers would make equivalent or larger savings through reduction in bills because the meters allow more detailed feedback on electricity use, and facilitate use of new flexible pricing tariffs with cheaper consumption at particular times of day (called 'time of use' tariffs). The AMI programme officially finished at the end of 2013, and a rebate was offered to customers if smart meter installation had still not been attempted at their property by the end of June 2014 (VAGO 2015: 29).

The AMI programme was subject to widespread criticism. There were large increases in customer bills, escalating installation costs, and a range of technical problems. This resulted in a number of consumer protests, including the forma-tion of a Stop Smart Meter Australia protest group as well as a political party – People Power Victoria – with the sole mandate of halting the implementation of smart meters. A lack of public sector leadership was also criticised heavily by the Victorian Auditor-General, who was called in to review the AMI in 2009, and again in 2015. So, despite the initial optimism around Victoria providing a positive 'best practice' demonstration of a new electricity metering policy for the rest of Australia to follow (see, for example, National Smart Metering Program 2008: 4; Marchment Hill Consulting 2009), the AMI programme emerged instead as a policy failure. From 2013 onwards there was a flurry of Australian federal and state government documents explicitly stating that the AMI programme would not be replicated elsewhere (see, for example, NSW Minister for Resources and Energy 2014; Department of State Growth 2015).

The policy failure of the AMI programme contributed to a change of policy at the national level in Australia: Australia's electricity metering policy changed quite significantly in the period 2013–2015, with a much less stringent and more open-ended policy of voluntary, competitive or 'market-led' smart metering installation introduced to the national electricity market in late 2018 (Australian Energy Market Commission (AEMC) 2012; Department of Industry and Science (Australia) 2015). In essence, the new Australian policy means there is no longer an obligation for advanced meters to be installed (AEMC 2015), and, indeed, several organisations have questioned whether there will be any significant customer uptake (see, for example, TasNetworks 2015).

The Victorian AMI programme highlights the challenges inherent in successfully constructing and leading complex collaborative projects. The private sector played an integral role in the AMI programme delivery: utility distribution companies were the main type of organisation contracted to implement the AMI programme, with the state government providing oversight. However, it was the nature of this relationship – and the lack of public sector leadership – that was criticised heavily by the Victorian Auditor-General. The institutional memories held about the project centre around this negative perception, an issue to which we now turn: first, examining how the Victorian smart metering policy was built on past ways of knowing; and, second, how it is represented now, including the methods by which representations of the past have been embedded (or not) within institutionalised processes.

When Memory Is Held by Others

The AMI programme centred on what was at the time new technology. Digital smart meters were not available in the late 2000s 'off the shelf' but were made specifically for Victoria. Thus there were few, if any, past ways of knowing in relation to this type of electricity meter. Further, the newness of the technology limited the number of organisations and people who were able to participate in conversations about the AMI programme – the plurality of voices was constrained.

One way of gathering information was to look spatially, rather than historically, at other countries who had implemented new meters. The Victorian government did this, for example, through commissioning studies on innovative metering in California and Italy (Essential Service Commission 2004): jurisdictions at the forefront of smart metering internationally.

Because of the newness of the technology, there was recognition that the state government was not in possession of as much knowledge as the private sector, because it was the utilities and metering companies who were actively developing new meters and were at the forefront of innovation. Although past ways of knowing were overall very limited, it was industry who had what little knowledge there was. As a policy advisor from an NGO explained:

(INTERVIEWER: Do you feel there were situations in which the industry held the knowledge around the technology? Or, there was technology-specific knowledge that was a resource to them, as it were?)

> This is the fundamental problem in all energy policy, not just a project like this: the industry has all the expertise. The government doesn't. The regulator doesn't. The consumer sector doesn't. We have some people in the consumer sector who have a fair bit of technical expertise and there are obviously some people in government and the regulator who have some technical expertise. But as a rule the industry is, like, they've got it all. They understand how the industry works more than anybody else so it does give them an advantage in getting things to go their way. And I think that's part of the governance challenge in energy policy generally, and a project like this in particular. (Interview)

A former director of the state government's AMI programme described the process: 'This [was] government trying to pick winners to some extent as to what's technically viable and what technologies might or might not work. We know that that's generally very sort of prone to mistakes I guess, or just being behind or not doing what the market might do' (interview).

This imbalance in technical knowledge about the meters between the public and private sector is cited by several interviewees as the reason why the state government set up the AMI programme but then delegated most of the responsibility of implementation to the private sector utilities, in the process constraining the plurality of voices and organisations actively participating in the programme: '[In] the first phase of AMI ... the whole process was very industry-centric ... Mostly the industry who had a direct interest in it, the retailers and distributors ... it was seen as a technical issue.' (interview). And, as the interviewee states, the government viewed the AMI programme initially as a relatively straightforward technical issue – centred on the new metering technology – again most probably in large part because of its lack of experience and past ways of knowing. As a consumer advocate explained:

> And so what the Victorian government did was ... they went ahead with a mandated roll-out after developing a business case which proved to be a very over-optimistic picture of what the actual cost of rolling out smart meters would be. And they jumped ahead of having a policy framework put in

place for consumer protections around smart metering and all of the prepara-
tory stuff to, all right, we'll roll them out as a technical reform.

They experienced the same lesson that I think absolutely everybody that
does a mandated meter roll-out makes the same mistake and has the same
observation and I've heard it said a few times . . . 'At the start we thought that
this was a technical reform but we realise now it is actually a social reform.
And in treating it as a technical reform we got the social side of it wrong.'
That's a common refrain that keeps coming up. (Interview)

It was only later recognised that there were a host of important social policy
issues associated with digital meter installation, such as increasing ease of
electricity disconnections for vulnerable low-income households and a flat-
rate increase in metering charges across all households, regardless of income
(St Vincent de Paul Society and Alviss Consulting 2016).

Representing and Remembering the Victorian AMI Programme

In the Victorian AMI case the dominant narrative – and how it is remembered –
is as a policy failure: the AMI provided a good story, and therefore encouraged
dynamic modes of memory transfer, through use of narrative, at conferences
and events and in the media. For example, there were twenty-four news articles
on the AMI in the Melbourne-based newspaper *The Age* in the period
2009–2013) (Lovell 2017). Different policy actors each describe the AMI in
negative terms:

In Victoria they had the mandatory roll-out of electricity smart meters, but
I doubt that's going to be repeated in any other states. (Interview)

My understanding is that the political support for smart meters just
whittled and whittled away until about 2011 or 2012 . . . the Victorian
experience was seen as extremely expensive with very limited and speculative benefits. I remember a senior Victorian government official saying to me,
'Victoria got on the smart meter bus, we looked around and where is
everyone?' . . . Victoria took the lead and then everyone bailed out on them.
(Interview)

We learnt from a negative perspective what not to do, I guess, from the
meter roll-out in Victoria. (Interview)

The criticism of the AMI programme included the Victorian Auditor-General,
who in the introduction to his second report on the AMI described the AMI as
follows: 'The reality of the smart meter rollout is that the state approved
a program, many of the costs of which it could not directly control, nor drive
many of the benefits ascribed to it' (VAGO 2015: viii). Once this negative
narrative formed, it appears to have been hard to shift. Thus narratives are
a characteristic of more dynamic forms of memory, but are not necessarily

themselves dynamic. The negative AMI programme narrative has to date been resistant to change. How did it become so embedded? The change in government in Victoria in 2010 from Labour to a coalition (Liberal/National) government certainly played a role in solidifying the narrative. After the election the new coalition government requested a review of the AMI programme, raising the possibility that it would halt its implementation, or significantly alter it (see Victorian State Government 2015). However, the new government did decide, rather reluctantly, to proceed, albeit with notable modifications including introducing optional flexible pricing, establishing a Ministerial Advisory Council, and subsidising in-home energy displays (see Victorian State Government 2015). The new energy minister explained the decision:

> Analysis shows that if you were looking at it from a blank sheet of paper you probably wouldn't go down this [AMI programme] path. There are actually more detriments to consumers, or costs to consumers as the result of the project as a whole, compared to the benefits. But we're not starting with a blank sheet of paper. We're starting with the mess we've inherited from the Labor government. (O'Brien 2011)

The AMI case demonstrates how forgetting failure appears to be less likely when dynamic forms of institutional memory, such as narratives, predominate. Based on this Victorian case the memories of failure appear more likely to persist. There is evidence that it is the narrative of policy failure that has had an effect in influencing the rest of Australia's policy decision-making, as an interviewee close to the decision-making processes describes:

> We've now moved to the voluntary [meter] roll-out model . . . and it's a bit of an elephant in the room, but it's not particularly controversial to say that it is a pretty inefficient way to roll out smart meters, because it results in dribs and drabs of meters . . . and doesn't get to a position of saturation quickly enough to really capitalise on the benefits that smart meters have . . . The real underlying driver behind that change of reform is that no energy minister now wants to be responsible for saying, 'We're going to do the same thing Victoria did.' (Interview)

A problem with dynamic forms of institutional memory is that they are partial: the need for a clear, dominant narrative in the story means that things that don't fit get left out, in this case positive things to do with the AMI – the stuff that worked well. One interviewee, for example, spoke of the benefit of improved network voltage information that resulted directly from the AMI programme, and was larger than originally anticipated; however, these benefits have not been fully explored due to the predominantly negative attitudes towards the AMI programme:

Smart metering provides information, not just about consumption, but also about power quality, which is essential to the distribution businesses. It is really valuable. In fact, the distribution businesses have found better benefits in this regard than were anticipated . . . It's a big plus to them . . . It's probably one of those areas where if you were still running a programme, you would go back and say, right, now let's quantify this. Let's fully evaluate this. Does this displace other benefits that we're not achieving? (Interview)

There is some evidence from the AMI case that more traditional static forms of institutional memory (e.g. government archives) were not fully developed or populated, because of the policy failure. For example, interviewees who were in government at the time describe a lack of detail in archiving and poor processes of static memory formation:

(INTERVIEWER: And in terms of what happened earlier this year when the AMI programme officially closed down . . . are there a certain set of procedures that you'd go through at that point, in terms of wrapping up?)

Yeah . . . I'm just trying to think, what were they? I mean, I wasn't really directly involved in that. No, I just can't, I just can't really – I mean, there are a whole lot of internal procedures that you have to go through. What are you thinking of in particular?

(INTERVIEWER: Well, just the kind of nuts and bolts of how institutional memory is constructed. So, for instance, were there exit interviews with everyone leaving the programme? Where you sat down and recounted your version of what happened with the programme and the learnings and that sort of thing?)

Not really, no. I don't really think that happened, no. But I don't really want to say that that didn't happen. I mean yes, look there was – so, the official version, yes there were records that were created. (Interview)

One reading of this is that with increasing accountability and transparency of government there is a fear that the files could be subject to a freedom of information request. Thus it becomes no longer politically feasible to record the negative aspects of a policy in the formal archives because this material could be used to attack the government, or the public servants themselves. So, accountability could be acting as a causal driver of the selective amnesia. But there is also evidence that institutional memory was hampered by short-term appointments within the AMI team, as per Pollitt's (2000) decline thesis:

I think the knowledge has been lost to a very large degree. When I completed my contract ... I agreed to stay on for six months in another position to provide an opportunity for the department to wrest from me as much as they thought that they would need to know.

(INTERVIEWER: So when you stepped down from the AMI, you were still in government?)

I was still in government for six months on a short-term contract, and that was my negotiation with the department ... Effectively, I'll stay around and I'm available to say whatever, to write down, to do whatever you want. Largely, on an expectation of being asked to hand over knowledge really.

(INTERVIEWER: And how did that play out?)

Well, I think I was probably asked one question in the six months. The replacement person I would go for coffees with, but by and large it was not a structured handover of knowledge, nor was there note-taking or anything else. All activities that I would have been expected to have been involved in, I suppose. So I think government does struggle with capturing knowledge and history and retaining that in a way that can be useful for the future. I think that's absolutely the case. I just don't think that they have the tools, nor do I think that the executive or managers within departments necessarily understand the way in which that can be achieved. (Interview)

Further, there were inherent difficulties in implementing more traditional processes of institutional record-keeping because of the collaborative nature of the AMI programme, with the private sector utilities playing an integral role in the AMI programme delivery. Hence much of the memory resides in the private sector rather than strictly with the responsible government department. The state government at the outset almost completely delegated the implementation of the policy to private sector utilities, as an interviewee explained: 'I think government's view of the programme at the time [2006–2012] was that you can leave it completely to industry. It was a mandated roll-out [of smart meters] by [the electricity] distributor. They can do the whole thing themselves – we don't really have to have any involvement' (interview).

In the case of the AMI we therefore identify two elements of institutional amnesia: first forgetting of the things that worked well with the AMI (accidental or dynamic amnesia, lost through narrative formation), and, second, deliberate or static amnesia, stemming from failure to keep adequate records. Both types of memory loss have been facilitated by the absence of forum occasions wherein it was possible to have a plurality of voices heard, with both positive and negative aspects of the AMI programme fully discussed. The AMI programme simply became too politicised for this to be seen as desirable.

Preserving Rich Narratives from 'Successes' or 'Failures'

Processes of institutional memory in government are becoming more dynamic, in particular through use of narratives, iterative conversations and a plurality of voices. Our empirical case of the AMI programme in Victoria, Australia, is a case in which the narrative is one of failure. The situation was, and still is, one in which it is difficult to say anything positive about the AMI programme or learn from its successes, because it runs counter to the narrative. There is evidence of two types of amnesia in the AMI programme: dynamic amnesia (lost through narrative formation and subsequent silencing of positive voices), and static amnesia (failure to keep full government records).

One key policy issue raised here is about how to preserve positive aspects of predominantly negative stories. What is required is multidimensional, contested, messy and iterative narratives, as opposed to one-dimensional stories of policy failure such as we observe in the case of the AMI programme. In static modes of institutional memory formation each version of a document had to be saved so that the file is sedimented and embraced multiple perspectives and views. We need a similar process for dynamic modes of institutional memory formation, albeit while acknowledging that narratives do not naturally work that way. Ideally dynamic memories need to be multidimensional if they are going to guard against amnesia. One possible solution is to embrace dissident and critical internal voices, with managers being mindful of a plurality of opinion and experience. Conceptually, we need to focus our attention on better understanding the moments of narrative formation – whether through forums or other occasions – and thus how stories of policy failure might be influenced at particular points in time in order to include a plurality of voices, and hence a fuller account of both failure and success.

4 Differentiated Memories: The Case of the UK's Zero Carbon Hub

'Dynamic' Institutional Memories	Operationalised	Illustrative Case Study
Held in common across hybrids of actors	Physically locate people together in 'hubs', 'task forces' or 'steering groups' for portions of the policy process	Zero Carbon Homes, United Kingdom

One of the 'new orthodoxies' in the Anglo-European public administration literature is the claim that over the past three to four decades we have witnessed a shift from 'government to governance' (Rhodes 1996), with policymaking now being undertaken by a 'differentiated polity' (Marsh 2011). The key argument in this literature is that both executive decision-making and service delivery are increasingly networked, rather than hierarchical, with public sector institutions only one part of a complex mix of actors engaged in policymaking and delivery (Marsh and Rhodes 1992). There is considerable debate in this literature about the extent to which governments steer this process (Marsh 2011), but either way the trend towards forms of collaboration between government actors and indeed public and private sectors is clear.

If government institutions are only one actor in a policy network then we would expect that networked memories would function differently to institutional memories. The aim of this section is to show how memories can reside in a network rather than an institution – that is, they reside with the actors themselves who spend their career moving between institutions in the network (both public and private), with their memories a key part of their professional skill set. In this way the type of churn that Pollitt laments becomes a strength rather than a weakness of our more dynamic conceptualisation. It also points to how different types of governance institutions – namely 'hubs', 'task forces' or 'steering groups' – that physically locate people together for portions of the policy process can act to improve memories by providing for opportunities in which a shared language and set of experiences is created. Section 2 examines such a hub within the public sector, whereas in this section we examine a public–private collaborative hub. The common criticism of these types of initiatives is that the resultant memory is fragmented and disparate due to the churn of key staff. We show that this is not always the case.

As in previous sections, we use one primary example to illustrate this point – the UK's Zero Carbon Homes (ZCH) policy – but include illustrative links to the other three cases considered in this Element to reinforce our claims. ZCH was abandoned by the UK government in 2016. We do not seek to re-evaluate or revisit that discussion here (but see Lovell and Corbett 2018). Instead we focus on the role that the Zero Carbon Hub – a public–private partnership created to iron out technical details – played in the policymaking process, and highlight that there is a fairly consistent and stable memory about how the Hub came about, what it was designed to do, and what its strengths and limitations were. The key point is that when the UK government created a Zero Carbon Homes policy in 2006 it was because the coalition of actors, including a network of environmentalists and progressive home builders, had been advocates for some time. Their enthusiasm, knowledge and expertise was not dependent on government policy and so there is no reason we would expect it to dissipate when the government chose to abandon its intervention a decade later. As a result, the policy initiative could be revived should the priorities of the government change, even though the physical institution of the Hub has been abolished.

The Zero Carbon Homes Policy

The 1990s and early 2000s were active years for building sustainable homes in the UK. An internet-based survey reveals that over 150 sustainable and low-energy housing developments were built or planned in the UK in the period 1990–2004, comprising more than 24,000 dwellings (Lovell 2005). Most of these sustainable homes were built without government support. They can be characterised as bottom-up or grassroots developments, in the main initiated by individuals and organisations with strong sustainability values and desires (Lovell 2004, 2009; Seyfang and Smith 2007). Two zero carbon housing developments that gained a significant amount of media attention, and became more widely known outside of green homebuilding circles, were the Beddington Zero Energy Development (or BedZED) and the Hockerton Housing Development. BedZED, a low-energy development in South London, was completed in 2002.

Previous research has shown that the main motivation for the individuals and organisations active in the UK during the 1990s and early 2000s for initiating and building these sustainable homes was to enable a material demonstration that they worked (Lovell 2007); in other words, to show that it was possible – economically and technically – to build homes sustainably in the UK. The material existence of the homes was hence key to giving confidence and credibility to those advocating housing as a way of mitigating climate change (along with other sustainability problems). The low energy and low carbon housing that was constructed was mostly conceived of, and certainly acted, as tools or devices designed to shape ideas and practices. With the rise of climate change as an issue on the UK policy agenda during the 1990s (Toke 2000), it was valuable to have material evidence of low-carbon practice in order to promote new ideas and gain policy support, at a time when government was looking for solutions (Lovell 2004).

The deliberate use of already existing zero carbon homes to enhance the credibility and salience of policy narratives was an effective strategy: these activities caught the attention of the UK government. BedZED in particular was identified by the UK government as an attractive solution to a host of policy problems (Lovell 2004), acting as a focal point for policymakers interested in developing credible solutions to resolve difficult policy problems, in particular climate change, where the UK government had made a number of policy commitments (Department of Trade and Industry (DTI) 2003). In other words, the material existence of this zero carbon housing is a critical reason why policymakers wished to be associated with it, because it was judged to be proof that the ideas and technologies embedded in the dwellings worked, thereby giving instant credibility to what otherwise might have been dismissed as rhetoric.

In 2006, then Housing Minister Ruth Kelly announced that 'Our key goal is to achieve zero-carbon new homes within a decade' (Department for Communities and Local Government (DCLG) 2006: 1). In a speech at a green building event hosted by the environment group World Wide Fund for Nature (WWF), Housing Minister Kelly explained how 'It is vital that homes and other buildings are as sustainable and as eco-friendly as possible . . . Within a decade I want every new home to be zero-carbon . . . This country is the first to set this ambition and we look forward to our international partners matching it.'

The 2006 policy document *Building for a Greener Future* (DCLG 2006) set out three main ways in which the zero-carbon target would be achieved: through the planning system; through the building regulations (via Part L, which relates to energy); and through a voluntary, sustainable building standard – the Code for Sustainable Homes. Interim steps for Part L of the Building Standards were proposed: a 25 per cent improvement on energy use on current building regulations by 2010, and a 44 per cent improvement by 2013. Care was taken to specify what was meant by a zero carbon home: 'For a new home to be genuinely zero carbon it will need to deliver zero carbon (net over the year) for all energy use in the home – cooking, washing and electronic entertainment appliances as well as space heating, cooling, ventilation, lighting and hot water . . . It could be at the development or building level' (DCLG 2006: 15). However, this definition also preserved some flexibility over how 'zero carbon' was to be interpreted and implemented, i.e. at the 'development or building level'. The ZCH policy had multiple, ambitious policy aims: the zero carbon home would mitigate climate change, but also 'driv[e] innovation in the market and reduc[e] costs of technologies' (DCLG 2006: 1), facilitate the building of new homes, and reduce fuel poverty. The key challenge the ZCH policy faced was matching the ambition of 'zero carbon' with the practicalities of housebuilding. This required a technical solution. The Zero Carbon Hub ('the Hub') was created to provide it.

Creating the Hub

The Hub was essentially a public–private partnership between government and industry designed to iron out the technical aspects of achieving 'zero carbon' homes. The Hub was the brainchild of key industry insiders. It was formally constituted in mid-2008. Its board of directors mirrored the mix of stakeholders and it had a small permanent staff responsible to a managing director. To make it work the Hub had to maintain a clear identity: it wasn't a policymaking body but rather had a research and implementation function. Interviewees reflected that the fact that no one stakeholder had control of the Hub made this possible and allowed for the recruitment of independently minded people who were problem focused.

The key issue for the Hub was to determine what 'zero carbon' meant in practice. Specifically, industry was concerned that what it meant was a dramatic increase in the cost of building new homes without a corresponding increase in sales premiums, as one interviewee explained:

> [It became clear to many of us] that it wasn't necessarily as straightforward an objective to achieve as they [government] perhaps initially thought. Because after all, nobody had real experience of trying to do this and exactly what was involved and what the stumbling blocks might be ... You put it all out together and I think there was a recognition across the board that this was a trickier assignment than people perhaps initially thought it was. And the idea of the Hub was to create a kind of implementation body, not a policymaking body, that could actually help all of the parties work together on a trusted basis like creating an independent, neutral space to work out what exactly needed to be done, technically and otherwise, to take the policy forward. (Interview)

The long lead-in time for the policy made this possible and so the Hub's main task was to square this circle: to get to a point where homes could meet a zero carbon specification without a major increase in costs.

The original definition of zero carbon referred to all energy uses in the home: both for heating (the traditional building regulations focus) and appliances. By 2010 this was watered down to just heating. The Hub reached these compromises by drawing together task groups – on the Fabric Energy Efficiency Standard, on Carbon Compliance and on Allowable Solutions. Key to each was the secondment of technical experts from different industries who were paid by industry to work on the technical aspects of the policy. This was important because their salaries were often far higher than the average civil servant but the work they were doing was essential to the successful implementation of the policy.

Virtually everybody that we interviewed agreed that the Hub was a successful model and many hold it up as an example of best practice:

> It worked really well, I think. I mean, it was a really successful body in its heyday. While there was a feeling – I think industry got behind it because they felt that government were interested in them ... that helped get UKGBC

[United Kingdom Green Building Council] off the ground as well, if we're being honest, because there was a sense that government were listening to us . . . It was quite powerful. And when industry is feeling like government is taking it seriously and listening – they've kind of set out the direction of travel but they are listening to the cautions and the advice. Then people love it. (Interview)

In addition to government interest, interviewees identified the following strengths of the hub approach. Following Pollitt's argument that civil servants are increasingly generalist because they rotate rapidly within and between public sector institutions, the Hub brought together and created genuine expertise. Subsequently, the experts won legitimacy among different stakeholders by providing detailed and rigorous analysis that was widely accepted as impartial. But, unlike a typical consultancy, these ideas were rigorously debated and tested, usually via the task groups. It therefore provided a platform for learning among and between stakeholders. The impending deadline meant that there was a single direction of travel or objective with a clear timeline for implementation. This ensured that even sceptical stakeholders remained involved in the process and could eventually be convinced of its value. The commitment of key staff to the process meant that the Hub became the repository of memory on this topic despite churn among the civil service and ministers.

The Hub as an Incubator of Memories

The strengths of the Hub provide clues as to the capacity of networks to capture and disseminate memories. The key is understanding that memory resides with the *actors* rather than the institution. This is illustrated by what happened to the Hub when the Zero Carbon policy was abandoned by the Conservative government in 2015. In the first instance, standard institutional archiving procedures were followed, with industry setting money aside to maintain an e-repository of the Hub's policy and technical publications. But the limitations of this static view of memory were clear to many interviewees:

Well, there are an awful lot of reports written by the Zero Carbon Hub. I don't know what's going to happen to those. That's a slight worry that in five years' time they disappear from the websites. They're up there at the moment . . . (Interview)

It may be the NHBC [National House Building Council] take over the records, because they were the driving force behind the Hub . . . if anybody has the collective records of that it would be them . . . As far as I'm aware, [the government took] no responsibility for recording what was going on.

Another vehicle can be . . . [parliamentary] select committees. If they did a study it would be properly recorded and their conclusions written up. So, if you formalise it in that way you might record the views at that time . . . The Hub's thoughts on all these issues were written up. Not only on performance gap but on things like overheating, ventilation. There was work done, and it was written up. So, the material is there, it's just not moving forward any longer. (Interview)

The point about government being uninterested in the memory of these policy initiatives is echoed by a former senior civil servant:

On the whole an ambitious civil servant prides themselves on acquiring knowledge of an area and then rapidly moving on. It's part of the way you get promoted. So even if you didn't have the kind of massive reductions we've all experienced in our civil service, you would still have an issue of retaining memory. That's why I say I think that it's much easier for people who are experts to pursue their expertise through other organisations [such as arm's-length or peak industry bodies]. (Interview)

The upshot, as we have seen in previous sections, is that the traditional static conception of institutional memory does not provide tools for effectively capturing this kind of dispersed memory, despite its centrality in practice to processes of policy learning.

By contrast, if we take a dynamic view we can appreciate that the networked approach means that memory resides in the sector and the key actors involved, rather than documentary reports, files or archives. There are obviously strengths and limitations in thinking of memory as sectoral rather than governmental. One strength is that industry has more incentive to remember than government. Indeed, ministers recalled that when they first came to a particular policy area they often felt that key lobbyists knew more about the topic than they did, as this former UK housing minister reflects:

When a minister changes, all the lobbyists . . . will immediately seek to engage with that minister in one way or another, and a sensible minister will want to do the same . . . You can't move an inch in [some] policy areas without hearing exactly what people think about that, and also advocating the things that you should be doing, in their opinion. (Interview)

In this view, entrenched interests are an important vehicle for institutional memory, for better or worse. Indeed, reflecting sectoral interest, once government funding dried up the Hub continued with funding from industry:

There's so much private money that could go into this stuff so they're not going to do it alone. And it doesn't actually – it almost doesn't need the public sector money. In fact, that Zero Carbon Hub, once the government pulled its funding about three years ago, the private sector continued to fund it because it felt it was important. Gradually it was like, 'Well, no one's listening to this body anyway, let's just disband it.' And so it almost doesn't need public money, although that helps, because it means they've got a stake in it. It needs the interest of whatever minister it may be. (Interview)

The privately funded Hub had different incentives to the public–private partnership, however, as a former director explained:

> When the Hub finished, I formed another company called The Buildings Hub, and that still runs today. It's still doing much of the work that the Zero Carbon Hub did, with the same operational directors, the same technical director, the same project director, [and] myself as managing director. We still carry on that work. (Interview)

The key difference is the Hub was no longer recognised as an independent organisation:

> We have to be a commercial operation. So we're no different than any other consultant ... So even though we tried to retain, and we have the support of the boards to retain, the principles of the journey, and working with government – I still go in to see the officials of the department, and I still get the same welcome and recognition as a voice. I have an open door: 'Come and see us any time you like.' I still can't move on with anything practically because we have to be a commercial organisation now, and that was fundamental. (Interview)

Nevertheless, the fact that the network persists means that the policy could be revived relatively quickly should government interest return:

> Industry was up for re-forming it if the government changed its policy back to it, and it still would. Industry would still support a Zero Carbon Hub organisation if government still asked for it, I believe. (Interview)

Indeed, there has been discussion within the industry about whether other parts of government, like the Greater London Area, would still pursue zero carbon targets. In which case, the narratives persist within the sector despite the 'temporary blip' (interview) in national government interest, and this is a key strength of having memories that reside in networks of actors rather than institutions.

Interviewees conceded that the key weakness of having memory reside in the network, and held by industry in particular, is that their main goal is to maximise profit:

> Well, the trouble is from the private sector's perspective ... they just think about it as how it affects them as an individual company. I mean, UKGBC [UK Green Building Council] arguably would be a good repository for this information, but we [would] need funding and somebody to pull it all together

and the time to do it ... At the moment it's kind of all fresh in our brains so we're not seeing the need to write it down. (Interview)

More generally, as the final sentence of the above quote illustrates, dynamic memories that are actor centred only last as long as the people concerned are active in the network. Once they move on the memory is lost, unless it is actively retold or narrated to new entrants into the profession. And yet, it is less clear how much worse this is than having detailed archival files that are never read because a new generation of policymakers does not know they exist. In which case, both static and dynamic memories tend to have a limited life span. But recognising their networked nature can allow us to *work with* the nature of modern government rather than against it.

Networked Memories

The UK Labour government initiated the Zero Carbon Homes policy in 2006 but the impetus for change came from the sector driven by environmental activists but also sympathetic industry stakeholders who anticipated the shifting policy direction and sought regulatory certainty from government. This sector and the network of actors who work within it thus existed well before the 2006 policy and they persist after it. They have memories that are passed down to new entrants via socialisation in different institutional settings. But they also move between these institutions and so have a shared, collective memory about policies like Zero Carbon Homes and a narrative about why it succeeded or failed, and a sense of where it fits in the broader landscape of housebuilding regulation in the UK.

This collective memory is inherently dynamic. There are some files and records. There are web archives. But by and large memory resides with the people involved. This has both strengths and weaknesses. The strength is that the memory is not dependent on government attention and enthusiasm, which, as we saw, waxes and wanes depending on who is in power. The weakness is that the only way for the memory to continue beyond the working lives of the actors involved is for it to be passed down as a form of oral history to new entrants. This reliance on socialisation means that memory is often fragmented, with no single, authoritative rendering of the story.

Physically locating people together in 'hubs', 'task forces' or 'steering groups' for portions of the policy process is one way of getting around this problem. Section 2 shows the success of this approach through the case of the cross-government family violence policy hub that was established in Tasmania, Australia. As we have seen with the UK Zero Carbon Hub, the story about how it was created, what it set out to do, and its strengths and limitations is fairly consistent across the people we interviewed. Many of the same people were involved for its lifespan and they have co-produced a narrative that makes clear what the fault lines between groups were and how the process of discussion and dialogue enabled them to be overcome. As a result, despite the cessation of the 2006 Zero Carbon Homes policy, the Hub persists in a new form, ready to be reactivated in the future.

To be sure, it may well be that the way the Hub is remembered owes a lot to the fact that it was almost universally viewed as a success. We could certainly imagine how more controversial 'hubs' might lead to a more contested narrative, with memory fragmented and fractured in much the way critics of a dynamic approach highlight. Determining why some such attempt to physically locate people together works to create a stable and positive memory, and others don't, is not our aim here. Rather, we simply use the Hub to illustrate that the supposed drawback of this type of dynamic memory is not predetermined; a Hub-type model is not perfect but it has the distinct advantage of being highly attuned to the processes and practices of modern government.

5 Living Memories: The Case of the New Zealand Justice Sector

'Dynamic' Institutional Memories	Operationalised	Illustrative Case Study
Stored as 'living' memories through a combination of fresh perspectives, individual agency and shared stories	A core rhetorical device that represents shared understandings, and reminds participants about key elements of networked memory	The justice sector, New Zealand

The previous section argued that, as public administration has shifted from government to governance, similarly memory has shifted from being held by a single institution, to being distributed across a network of actors. This section considers a related aspect of how modern dynamic institutional memory is conceived differently to the older static view; in particular, that memory includes 'living' memories of actors, in addition to archival records.

The information stored within the living memory of networked actors tends to differ qualitatively from the information stored in archival records. Records are suited to the retention of facts and figures, and tend to include 'official' and potentially censored accounts of what happened and why. The memories of the various actors often include less factual detail, but more frank judgements about what worked and what didn't, forming narratives of the process.

Living memory does not stay still, because lessons are always in the process of being recontextualised. What is the most salient lesson from a past experience must be updated with each new experience. In this respect we describe living memories of government policies as a combination of individual memories, shared understandings, and fresh perspectives, that update and augment our understanding of the past.

Living memories are remembered, accessed and transmitted through mechanisms that differ from static archival records. These memories tend to be stored and transmitted in the form of narrative and stylised accounts of what happened (stories), or further in parables, fables, metaphors and other rhetorical devices. This section describes the use of metaphor in the storage and transmission of living memories in the New Zealand 'justice sector'.

The New Zealand Justice Sector

New Zealand was a leader of the 'new public management' reforms of the 1980s (Boston et al. 1996). With these reforms came a focus on strict, vertical, single-point accountability; public managers each have responsibilities for delivering a defined set of public services to a required quality and quantity (Boston et al. 1996). Government was also divided into a large number of mostly single-purpose agencies, with many problems falling between or across multiple agencies (Schick 1996). These two factors exacerbated the challenges of inter-agency collaboration, and many of New Zealand's most persistent policy problems were those that spanned the responsibilities of multiple agencies (Scott and Bardach 2019).

The New Zealand government responded with a series of initiatives designed to get agencies to work together more effectively (Scott and Macaulay 2020). One such initiative was Managing for Outcomes (Scott and Boyd 2016a), which encouraged government agencies to describe how the outputs that they produce contributed to end outcomes (through intervention logic). Where the outputs of multiple agencies produced a combined effect, these agencies were encouraged to form committees to discuss and coordinate how they could 'manage for shared outcomes' (Baehler 2003). One committee concerned the relationship between criminal justice policy, policing, courts and corrections. Officials from the Ministry of Justice, New Zealand Policy, and the Department of Corrections began to meet regularly in 2003 and 2004 to develop shared intervention logics in order to fulfil their reporting requirements under the Managing for Outcomes initiative. Similar groupings were formed across government, but most were disestablished as central agencies stopped actively promoting Managing for Outcomes in 2005 (Jensen et al. 2014).

However, the justice sector continued and went from strength to strength. By 2012 the justice sector was being seen as one of the more effective examples of interagency collaboration. The Government tasked the Justice Sector Board (the new name for the chief-executive-level committee) with reducing over five years the crime rate by 15 per cent and the criminal reoffending rate by 25 per cent (Scott and Boyd 2016b, 2020). This focus on outcomes placed new pressure on the justice sector to work together and innovate.

The justice sector knew that it couldn't achieve the broader social changes needed to reduce crime and criminal reoffending on its own. For some time, the three core agencies had coordinated with the smaller Serious Fraud Office and Crown Law Office, as well as the part of the Ministry for Social Development that was responsible for child protection (Scott and Boyd 2015). Taking this approach one step further, the justice sector is now working with other government departments to implement the processes it has used. For example, it is coordinating with the Ministry of Transport on reducing traffic-related crimes, the Ministry of Health on ensuring that addiction and mental health services are coordinated with criminal justice activities to prevent crime, and various social and educational services to help offenders to reintegrate into society and reduce the likelihood of reoffending.

The Pipeline Metaphor

Business analysts from the three justice sector agencies worked to better understand and plan for annual business activity. Interviewees recall that from 2003, public servants began to refer to a 'justice sector pipeline', which showed how changes in criminal justice policy (by the Ministry of Justice) affected policing activity (by New Zealand police), which in turn affected the demand on the various courts (Ministry of Justice) and correctional facilities (Department of Corrections). The 'pipeline' metaphor was used to convey the concept of linear dependency, with 'upstream' decisions having 'downstream' effects. This metaphor went on to become a critical part of the living memory narrative about the New Zealand justice sector.

While most of the Managing for Outcomes committees were either disestablished or evolved into very different forms, the 'justice sector' (as the three agencies were then informally known) continued to meet. The pipeline metaphor provided a single-word *raison d'être*. As one senior manager put it, 'One of the things that binds the justice sector together more than any other sector is this idea of the pipeline, the idea that people flow through the system. So, there's no manufactured sector here … It's clear and it's evident and it's pressing' (interview).

Over time, the pipeline metaphor took on other meanings. It became associated with custodial chain management – the transfer of offenders between the police, the courts and correctional facilities. The pipeline was no longer just the flow of work demands created by upstream decisions – it had come to represent the literal pathway of individuals from a police cell to a police transport van to a courtroom to a corrections transport van, and so forth. Each transition involved time, labour and cost.

Between 2005 and 2012, the justice sector engaged in a number of discrete projects, but also met regularly to discuss areas of mutual interest. Governance arrangements were progressively formalised, with the introduction of terms of reference, a tiered structure (monthly meetings of chief executives, fortnightly meetings of their deputies) and a formal secretariat ('Sector Group'). Sector Group was a jointly resourced team consisting of staff from each of the three agencies, co-located at the Ministry of Justice to work on areas of mutual interest.

It was around this time that the agencies started to work together to intentionally manipulate the pipeline. Earlier efforts had tried to understand the pipeline so that agencies could plan with greater accuracy, based on understanding how upstream actions would have downstream impacts. But it was also apparent that downstream pressures could be better managed by upstream investments. The Justice Sector Fund, first created in 2012, was a novel financial tool that allowed accumulated underspends in one part of the pipeline to be spent in other areas. The Justice Sector Fund allowed, for example, the Department of Corrections to invest in services delivered by other agencies to reduce the number of prisoners in correctional facilities, or for agencies to jointly invest in new approaches to custodial chain management. For example, one such innovation was the use of audio-visual links in courts and prisons that allowed offenders to attend procedural hearings without needing to be physically transferred out of the prison, into a transport van, into a court, and back again.

As this Element is being written in 2019, the justice sector has been in operation for sixteen years, and continues to operate as a tightly knit collaborative arrangement between separate agencies. During that time, each role within the justice sector has been carried out by many different people. Some have moved on to other government positions related to crime and criminal justice, others have moved to different agencies, and some have left the public service entirely. Despite this turnover, the justice sector has retained as its unifying concept the metaphor of a pipeline, through which offenders pass.

Encoding Living Memory

Linde (2009) described how institutional memory often takes the form of a story or stories. Humans have been characterised as a 'storytelling animal' (Gottschall 2012), and make sense of their lives by thinking about them in story or narrative form (Bruner 1990). Storytelling has been of increasing interest in the social sciences since the 1970s (Czarniawska 2017; see White 1973 as an early notable example).

Organisational theorists propose that stories have explanatory value for the existence and practice of organisations; stories 'do not exist merely *in* organisations, but are instead *constitutive* of the organisation (Frandsen, Kuhn and Lundholt 2016: 2, emphasis in original). Under this view, organisations are storytelling systems that perform themselves into existence (Boje 1991a, 1991b). Storytelling may be particularly relevant to living memory, as most oral transfer of memory is structured in this way.

Stories may represent literal events (an account that provides a sense of causality and order; Frandsen et al. 2016), or may be intended to represent something that has been learned. In this latter case, stories may not be literally accurate, but instead are intended to help the receiver of the story to understand a concept that has been interpreted by the teller as instructive. If stories are interpreted as the transmission of knowledge and insights, rather than of literal history, this affords a much wider array of narrative forms and rhetorical devices. Lessons-as-stories may be presented as if they were factual accounts, or they may be presented as obviously fictionalised accounts that convey the same message, as parables and fables. Or, in the case of the New Zealand justice sector, lessons can be remembered and transmitted as metaphors.

Metaphors allow institutional memory to be transmitted through associations. Kohonen (2012) notes that humans store information about past events (memories) through associations with other analogous events. A metaphor is a method for transmitting information through reference to something else. More formally, metaphor is a method of understanding one conceptual domain in terms of another conceptual domain (Kovecses 2005). Metaphor and analogy do not imply that the other conceptual domain is identical, but that their features are similar in qualified ways (Nguyen and Umemoto 2012). It is a 'set of systematic correspondences between the source and the target' (Kovecses 2005: 104). An alternative definition is to consider metaphor as the transformation of information from a relatively familiar domain to a relatively less familiar domain (Tsoukas 1991). In the context of institutional memory, metaphor functions as a cognitive or communicative 'shortcut', in that large amounts of information about the less familiar domain can be stored by association with the familiar domain. Metaphors are therefore useful to the extent that the transformation of information is apt (the amount of transferable information is large) and that the qualifications or limitations on this transformation are understood.

Some authors have focused on the transfer of historical analogies based on their literal similarity to the current situation (Brändström, Bynander and 't Hart 2004). Others are more interested in more fanciful likenesses, like referring to policies as 'platforms' (Gaddefors 2007), the finance system as 'clogged' (Nguyen and Umemoto 2012), and organisations as biological entities (Czarniawska 2017). Or indeed, in the New Zealand justice sector, the flow of offenders is described as a 'pipeline'.

Metaphor as a Reminder of Shared Understandings

The New Zealand justice sector is one of the longest-lasting examples of interagency collaboration in the New Zealand public service. After sixteen years it continues to be a vibrant example of collaborative practice, despite all of the key leaders having changed several times over. The interviews conducted in researching this Element included leaders from each of the agencies, as well as those who worked at each phase of the justice sector. Some were current leaders, but others have been out of the justice sector for almost ten years. What was most remarkable about the interviews was how consistent the descriptions were for how and why the justice sector was successful. The 'pipeline' metaphor was a large part of this commonality, raised by nine out of ten interviewees.

Those in the justice sector believe that it is effective in part because its participants understand their pressing need to work together. As one senior public servant described, '[Each sector] needs to work out, what are the things that will pull it together, what are the things that will keep it together, and what are the things that will transcend the personal relationships over time? When you do that you're kind of halfway there anyway' (interview). Others noted that having a shared metaphor was key to working together. The justice sector was 'assisted by having a fairly obvious pipeline' (interview), and 'a natural pipeline means that you're naturally linked together' (interview).

The 'pipeline' is, however, more than just a rationale for collaboration. It also provides explanations for how the justice sector should work together. That is, the best way to change outcomes might involve acting upstream: 'If you look at reoffending rates, there's an awful lot that the Corrections Department can do, but probably the biggest factor is what police do' (interview).

The interviewees could describe in detail how the 'pipeline' worked. But in conversation, the word alone was sufficient to reference these shared understandings. The different accounts, provided by senior public servants from different agencies involved in the justice sector over different periods, were remarkably similar, as demonstrated in these responses by five different interviewees:

> [The justice sector involves] a lot of moving parts and very much a pipeline in terms of how cases move through the system. (Interview)
>
> Somebody who would get arrested by New Zealand Police will be held by police, they might have to appear in court, so they'll get transferred to the court. Then if they get a custodial [order or sentence], they'll be remanded in custody, transferred to Corrections. (Interview)
>
> So, the criminal justice system pipeline starts very much in the policy area, then policing, and then courts, and then on to Corrections, so there's a natural synergy across the sector. (Interview)
>
> I think very much is about understanding how the pipeline operates, understanding how people come into the system, how they exit the system, what happens to them when they're in the system, and what are the different points of intervention we have. So from a policy perspective it's very much around that pipeline. (Interview)
>
> So, one of the kind of defining features of the justice system is the kind of pipeline, the fact that sentences are set, people commit crimes, they'll go through the police system, they'll then go through the court system. If they're found guilty, one way or another, they'll end up through the corrections system. (Interview)

Metaphor as 'Living' Memory

The 'pipeline' started as a description of the effect of policing activities on the prison muster, but came to convey a large amount of shared information. With a simple reference to the 'pipeline', often by that one word alone, participants in the justice sector reference shared understandings about the need for collaboration, a particular model of business planning, processes in custodial chain management, preventative investment, and approaches to reducing recidivism. Participants in the justice sector have a living memory of sixteen years of criminal justice collaboration embedded in a single symbolic reference. These understandings have been continually updated and augmented with new understandings.

In this respect, the 'pipeline' metaphor may be considered as a kind of 'boundary object'. Boundary objects are a construct from social psychology to describe an abstract of concrete object that inhabits different intersecting social worlds (Star and Griesemer 1989; Scott 2019). Key characteristics are that they satisfy the informational requirements of each social world, are plastic to the needs of the parties using them, and yet robust enough to maintain a common identity when used by different parties (Scott, Cavana and Cameron 2016). The 'pipeline' began as a specific reference to a single flow-on effect, but was plastic enough to incorporate fresh perspectives and new information, such that it came over time to reference large amounts of shared understanding.

In this section we present an example of the use of rhetorical device to encode and transmit shared understandings of leadership lessons as living memory – in this case, the use of the pipeline metaphor to 'pull [a group of agencies] together ... and keep it together' (interview), to share information and coordinate business planning, to optimise processes at points of intersection, and to invest at the point of greatest impact. This metaphor provided a rationale for collaboration, stored and transmitted institutional memory, and allowed this memory to be updated and augmented with fresh perspectives (through its plasticity as a boundary object).

This is not to say that other collaborative efforts should use the 'pipeline' metaphor, or even a metaphor at all. The pipeline was and is a useful metaphor for the justice sector because it is accurate and has descriptive power, it provides a rationale for ongoing working together, it provides some information about how the various agencies should work together, and it is flexible enough to be used to describe various aspects of the justice sector and to be updated with fresh perspectives. The metaphor is used so frequently that new members of the justice sector must quickly learn the shared understandings that it represents, and thus these shared understandings are perpetuated. Other collaborative efforts will need to encode their leadership insights through other narrative devices, whether they be a metaphor (as in this case), a fable, a story, or any other verbally communicated construct or rhetorical device that conveys a key lesson.

The pipeline concept was not created deliberately for the purpose of helping the justice sector to understand why and how to work together, but it has come to have that effect. It has come to be an important part of how the memory of the justice sector, and its lessons, are retained. Any account of dynamic institutional memory must include how such lessons are remembered, through the stories and abstract concepts that the participants share.

A permanent public service supports government by providing a repository of information about the past – facts and figures about historical events. But it also has a memory of leadership insights about how to work – for example, how to bring collaborative actors together around a shared purpose, or how to plan together to ensure that dependencies are accounted for. This kind of wisdom about the past tends not to be found in the archives but is nonetheless an important aspect of institutional memory. Instead, it is stored as living memory within the various actors, and is passed between public servants as stories, parables, fables and metaphors.

The New Zealand justice sector demonstrates that metaphors can be instrumental in the success of collaboration, and in remembering the leadership lessons of how to sustain that collaboration despite institutional churn (Stark 2019) and the passage of time. The selection and curation of such rhetorical devices is therefore, consciously or not, an important action in the development and retention of living memories.

6 Conclusion

The public policy literature of the past decade has begun to wrestle more explicitly with questions of what constitutes policy failure (King and Crewe 2013; McConnell 2015), and indeed what makes for a policy success (Compton and 't Hart 2019). The attention is both welcome and overdue. It offers new footholds into older debates about policy learning and new insights into how much politics and political compromise shape policy reality. As we have tried to show in this short Element, it also provides an opportunity to rethink institutional memory. Policy successes and failures have a long reach into the future because of the stories that are told about them. Those stories are in fact a form of institutional memory. They are carried by individuals and groups of actors and combine with documentary evidence to create dynamic narratives about 'what works'.

We began the Element by setting out 'the problem' of institutional memory. The literature is in agreement that institutional memory is in decline (Pollitt 2000, 2007, 2008, 2009; Wettenhall 2011; Rhodes and Tiernan 2014; Lindquist and Eichbaum 2016; Stark 2019). Less clear, but clearly implied, is that this perceived deterioration is detrimental to effective policymaking. These important observations essentially set up a deficit model of institutional memory. Factors like position churn, under-resourcing of information management systems, and increasingly distant relationships between public servants and political actors have created a memory-shaped hole in how government works. What impact this has on policymaking is something that itself requires further study.

If we accept that it's happening, and accept the characterisations thus far offered by the literature on *why* it's happening, where does that leave us? All of the factors ostensibly contributing to institutional memory loss have underlying drivers that mitigate against simple reversal. Technological change, for example, is driving the movement towards digitisation and forms of information management that have little to do with the static paper files of old. No amount of wishing is going to reverse that trend. It is simply now another 'new normal' of contemporary public management.

Similarly, position churn is here to stay. Older, hierarchical traditions in which civil servants would quietly work their way up the ladder, each waiting their turn in ways that build up a cumulative and predictable body of knowledge, are gone. All the incentives for an ambitious public servant are to keep moving, to shape a varied career and build as wide a body of skills as possible for them as an individual. It is almost certainly neither possible nor desirable to reverse this trend. Movement, of both ideas and people, is part of a healthy, outward-looking and open-minded bureaucracy. Lamenting the attendant loss of institutional memory does little to move the debate forward on how best to respond. If we accept the conventional 'static' view of memory, we are left with a deceptively simple question: what can we *do* to stop the loss of institutional memory?

A New Conceptualisation of Memory

Our argument here has been that lamenting the loss of institutional memory is based on a mis-characterisation of what memory is and what purpose it serves. Even in the mid-twentieth-century heyday of 'traditional' record-keeping, with paper files neatly stacked and labelled for posterity, there was not in fact an objectively cast 'memory' being stored. Just like other forms of data, documentary evidence does not speak for itself. It has life only through the interpretations of those who read it and make sense of it. So institutional memory has never just been about good record-keeping; it has also been about individual memories and the stories used to share them. That's why position churn is seen as such a contributing factor to the problem. The people we miss are the people who have been in an office for two decades that every newcomer seeks out to ask, 'How is this thing done around here?' This has very little to do with formal ways of knowing, although that person may well say, 'Have a look at this file from ten years ago.' It's a lived and living interpretation in which human memory combines with documentary evidence.

There is in the end no substitute for people, because humans are the storytellers. Files don't tell stories any more than electronic records tell stories. They are just pieces of information waiting to be understood through the exercise of human agency. But without those external sources, without their authoritative backing, there is no capacity for triangulation to distinguish between myth and the more plausible interpretations of what has occurred. So both the files, and the people to interpret them, remain at the core of institutional memory.

Which brings us back to our goal of asking what can be done if both those factors are in fact being irreversibly undermined.

We argue in this Element that a fundamental part of the answer to this question is to reconceptualise institutional memory by more accurately defining what in fact are the 'representations of the past' that actors draw on to *narrate* what has been learned when developing and implementing policy. When these narratives are embedded in *processes* they become 'institutionalised'. When viewed in this way, the problems of institutional memory loss become surmountable. The challenge becomes supporting the formation, preservation and transmission of the stories necessary for effective policymaking and implementation.

Dynamic Memory Operationalised

None of that is easy. But the case studies collected in this Element point to the possibilities for how it can be done and provide examples of what has actually been shown to work in practice. This Element provides empirical evidence to show that many of the debates and developments of the past two decades on how modern governance works in fact link directly to institutional memory. For example, the prevalence of 'network governance' (Rhodes 1997) is now widely accepted, but without explicitly realising that networks actually offer new opportunities for the spread of memories. Similarly, the literature on 'whole-of-government' working and 'joined-up government' is extensive, but barely touches on the implications of this for memory. The role of government contractors and the private sector in co-producing policy is also now widely understood, but without engaging with the consequences of this for the building and retention of institutional memory.

All four case studies demonstrate that network governance leads to networked forms of memory. In some cases, like the justice sector in New Zealand and the Tasmanian Family Violence Action Plan, the memory is embedded in perceptions of success gained from collective working. In the case of the Victorian smart meters, perceptions of failure spread through the network of stakeholders across Australia like some kind of cautionary tale. In the UK, zero carbon homes generated a more complicated memory, with some of the non-government participants in particular finding value by holding onto the lessons and sharing them with others.

A second finding could be summarised as: the closer the people, the tighter the memory. This is hardly a startling finding at one level, and yet it holds important insights. The proverbial 'water cooler' conversation becomes a metaphor for this type of storytelling. As Hollywood so often depicts, a group of friends who hang out together every day in their formative years create not just a tight bond, but shared memories that are reproduced decades later as stories of a 'golden age'. Part myth, part history, it is the weaving together of experience with sentiment, and rationality with emotion, that creates this composite sense of shared memory that can be retold slightly differently by each individual member of the group. It remains a live conversation.

Something less intense but not dissimilar happens when actors working in a policy area are not just told to work together but are co-located together as part of that process. The public service task force working on the Tasmanian Family Violence Action Plan, and the participants in the zero carbon homes hub in the UK, worked intensively together in a dedicated office space. This allowed for debates, rapid knowledge-sharing in real time, and consistent descriptions of the strengths and weaknesses of the process. In both cases, there was near universal acceptance by all involved that the process had been a success, but also shared awareness of the lessons to be learned. In Tasmania this included recognition that the kind of fast-paced process that worked well in one case was not necessarily easily replicable in other situations. It was also clear that it took a toll in workload and commitment terms that would not be sustainable in different topic areas and when working to longer time frames. And the UK case shows what happens when the drive of political support ebbs away in the face of competing priorities.

What the two cases do show is that jurisdictional size need not be an automatic barrier to this type of close working. The benefits found in Tasmania were replicated in the UK situation by focusing collected expertise in groups small enough to remain workable. But there is room for caution here. The policy topics being addressed, such as family violence, were not strongly contested policy areas. Arguments of course remain on whether the policy prescriptions adopted are the right ones, but there was little disagreement over the policy goals themselves – there was no wider push from interest groups or civil society in defence of the status quo. Self-evidently, that is not the case in many policy areas. This matters because it shifts the dynamics around both the size of the group of stakeholders to be consulted and the clarity of the political leadership on the issue.

The insight that memory is a social construct rather than an inherently rationalist exercise offers benefits, but it also offers challenges when the institutional memory becomes immune to evidence-based argument. What do we do when the memories cease to align or triangulate with the documentary evidence? It is part of the unique challenge of institutional memory within government institutions because they operate within a particularly political environment. Politics intervenes to amplify particular stories and embed views of their success or failure to the extent that they inhibit almost any future experimentation. We could take the poll tax in the UK as an example.[1] It damaged the Thatcher government so severely, and the story around it is one of complete failure, so that the memory

---

[1] The poll tax was a policy implemented by the UK's Thatcher government in the late 1980s. The intention was to update and simplify the collection of local rates by introducing a flate-rate tax to be levied on every adult. It was deeply unpopular and caused enormous political damage to the government. There is extensive writing on the poll tax, but for a good overview see King and Crewe (2013: 41–63).

allows no room for 'rational' debate. Parts of the process may have been sound, but the story of failure is such that an evidence-based assessment of what might be worth hanging onto is simply no longer possible. That's what memories of failure can do; they can shut down future debate by shaping a one-dimensional story.

The Victorian smart meters case shows how that can happen. It is rare that all parts of a policy process are a failure from start to finish. There are positives to be found and learned from that get obfuscated or even buried behind negative overall conclusions. In terms of policy design, for instance, there is little in the way the policy process for smart meters was originally structured that wouldn't widely be seen as pretty standard practice. There was a clear policy objective with the laudable goal that installing smart meters would encourage more efficient management of the electricity grid. As an intervention, it veers close to the kind of behavioural nudge approach that governments are increasingly favouring across the globe.

The roll-out of smart meters was supported by a public–private partnership that was a policy instrument of choice in the late noughties. Collaborative working to ensure the availability of the required technical expertise was also in place. All of these positives, though, simply get lost in the narrative that developed around the policy outcome. A kind of 'don't mention the war' impact stifles the practical utility of institutional memory for policy learning when the memory is blocked or even wilfully forgotten. And this has a compounding impact.

There is clearly an interplay here between learning, accountability, blame and memory. As a series of insights by Bovens, Schillemans and 't Hart et al. (2008) and Hood (2011) have demonstrated, accountability can quickly dissolve into blame games, leaving little apparent incentive to institutionalise those memories. The Victorian case study on smart meters demonstrates the relevance of that insight. There is a crossover between the narrative told about a process, and the political story told by both constituents and political parties. From a technical point of view, it is possible to claim the smart meter roll-out as a success. In a period of only four years, 2.8 million smart meters were installed, representing 93 per cent of homes and small businesses in Victoria. Large broadband roll-outs in both Australia and the UK would love to boast that level of achievement. There was clear alignment between the policy goal of installing an efficient metering system and the implementation that occurred.

What went wrong was the politics. Nobody had learned the lessons of the UK poll tax that household flat charges for anything (in this case electricity meters) are going to be inherently contentious. And it is tempting to speculate that no one will learn the wider lessons on the smart meter implementation in Victoria – because all aspects of it have been rolled into a composite memory of failure.

That memory is shared across the stakeholders involved to the extent that it has become embedded memory, not capable of being re-examined in the more dynamic conversation envisaged in other case studies. This points to the limitations of institutional memory and the distinction it retains from policy learning. It is possible to have clear institutional memories and yet learn nothing from them.

Buried within that more negative aspect is another sign for optimism. The Victorian case demonstrates just how effectively a policy story can act as institutional memory, and how far it can spread through the networked veins of modern government. It passes socially and is shared irrespective of the documentary evidence. A new employee joining the Victorian public service would not need to be shown briefing notes on the smart meter outcome in order to understand it. They would simply be socialised into that memory, which is carried both horizontally and vertically by the groups of actors involved.

The desirable normative end point of all this must surely be to achieve that same level of shared memory, but as more nuanced and iterative conversations, capable of continuing to evolve. Arguably this requires the marrying of individual memories and political narratives with forms of documentary evidence that are widely accessible. Is it possible to combine modern forms of digital record-keeping with the dynamism of living conversations to help policy evolve?

The New Zealand case of the justice sector offers some hope that this may indeed be possible. At its heart is the idea of collaborative working. It seeks to replicate the benefits of whole-of-government approaches but within subject boundaries that are more sustainable in the longer term. If whole-of-government approaches can bring short-term focus, a whole-of-justice-sector approach creates similar crossovers but with a wider remit not bound by the same inherent short-termism. The justice sector is also instinctively good at routine procedures for capturing information in ways that can support institutional memory. As the case study shows, here is an area of government that still takes minutes, briefing notes, statistical data and routines seriously.

But that alone is not the secret to the success. Police services everywhere are good at writing down crime reports. What makes the New Zealand model work is the combination of the documentary evidence with dynamic conversations, underpinned by forums for sharing that are more than just an annual conference. The structured meetings are so regular, and so genuinely cross-agency, that they take on some of the characteristics of the Tasmanian family violence task force and the UK's zero carbon homes hub. They are able to share both information and stories in real time, socialising the memories from across the sector in ways more likely to underpin policy learning.

Figure 1 summarises the arguments of this Element about how to operationalise the processes that support policy memory. These arguments are drawn from the four case studies, but are also somewhat speculative, in that no one case study embodies each argument. Nor do the case studies demonstrate that dynamic institutional memory can be intentionally created by following these steps. Nonetheless, they offer practitioners some clues as to where to start. We propose that civil servants should first commit to the task of remembering, and see institutional memory as an important facet of public sector leadership. As in Tasmania, teams should include old and new heads, and knowledge from a variety of actors distributed across the network. Groups should be co-located where and when possible, so that they can experience events together and reflect and make sense of those events, much like the Hub in the UK example. Storytelling helps form and refine collective understandings, and can be shared in forums akin to those created in Victoria. As in New Zealand, procedures and living documents can help connect stories with records, while rhetorical devices like analogy and metaphor help make sense of the captured information. We have set out the figure in linear fashion to suggest that there are some benefits to consciously and sequentially building an awareness of institutional memory into the planning of each new project. At the same time we recognise that policymaking seldom runs in linear fashion. Policymakers must remain adaptable and flexible in how to apply these steps.

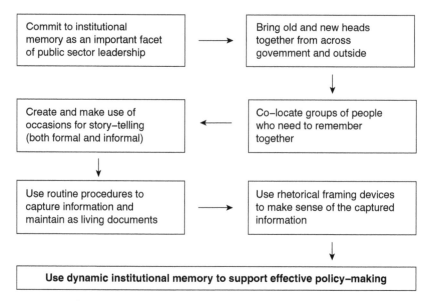

Figure 1 *Operationalising dynamic institutional memory*

Remembering Ahead

These case studies are of course merely indicative. We make no claims that they provide any definitive answers about contemporary institutional memory. What we do hope is that they provide some encouragement towards a wider new research agenda. The first aspect is in the area of closer testing of the causes behind the perceived deterioration in institutional memory, and widescale mapping of the spread and the impacts. The literature to date is long on arguments that institutional memory is diminishing but as yet too thin on establishing that as an empirical fact. The same can be said on the causes. The drivers identified so far make instinctive sense but require deeper empirical support. The correlation between changes in modes of governance and impacts on institutional memory seems clear; but correlation does not equal causation and more work is needed here.

The second aspect is in understanding how memory interacts with other jurisdictional factors. As policy memory is shared across a range of actors a multiplicity of forums can contribute to shaping that story. This might include industry bodies, academic networks and professional training bodies. There is some evidence in these four case studies that small jurisdictions are best placed to embrace more dynamic forms of memory, but this again is speculative and requires further research and testing. Similarly, there is insufficient understanding of how memory reacts with the system of government. Does memory travel better as a dynamic conversation within a federal state like Australia than it does in unitary systems? Does the more overtly political system of selecting bureaucratic leaders in the US presidential system impact on how memories are transmitted between organisational siloes?

Third, the relationship between documentary evidence and individual memory needs investigation. Do the two operate at distance from each other unless consciously brought together through the creative design of institutional structures? There is some evidence in our case studies that person-to-person knowledge transfer is still the most prevalent form, with people referring to other data sources only when pointed towards them. If both are in fact vital for a healthy, dynamic form of institutional memory to operate then greater understanding of the interaction between the two remains vital. Stories without sufficient evidential backing are misleading myths; but evidence without a narrative is just lines on a page – it is the two together that produce institutional memory. This Element has provided one set of arguments on how that interaction can work in a modern governance environment.

Fourth, the case studies in this Element illustrate, in hindsight, how memory was used in different policy cases. We cannot claim that replicating steps taken in each of these cases would lead to comparable results. And while the cases point to different practices for learning and telling stories, the toolkit available to practitioners is still relatively sparse. But this new dynamic perspective on institutional memory provides us with clues as to where we should look. If memory can be conceived as the telling of stories, backed by documentary evidence, we can begin to explore ways to preserve this dynamic interaction of story and evidence across any of the myriad ways that a modern governance environment might cause experiences to be forgotten or misremembered. This includes the causes of memory loss proposed in the static memory literature, like churn, digitisation, or the increased salience of distributed and networked actors. For example, if the fear is that memory is lost when individuals move from position to position, then we need to find ways to make sure they leave their stories behind when they go. And if the fear over documentary shortcomings is that vital insights get lost in mountains of inaccessible digitised data, then perhaps we need to create interactive systems capable of storing the plural accounts of past experience.

Static conceptions of memory have, to date, not led researchers towards workable solutions. It is our hope that in presenting this dynamic conception of memory we can orient researchers towards new avenues of exploration that will help institutions of the future to better remember the lessons of the past. The way institutional memory is conceived has been in need of a new story.

References

Alford, J. and J. O'Flynn. 2012. *Rethinking Public Service Delivery: Managing with External Providers*. Basingstoke: Palgrave Macmillan.

Australian Energy Market Commission (AEMC). 2012. *Power of Choice Review – Giving Consumers Options in the Way They Use Electricity*. Final Report. Sydney: Australian Energy Market Commission.

Australian Energy Market Commission (AEMC). 2015. *Rule Determination – Expanding Competition in Metering and Related Services*. Sydney: Australian Energy Market Commission.

Baehler, K. 2003. Managing for outcomes: Accountability and thrust. *Australian Journal of Public Administration* 62 (4): 23–34.

Bartenberger, M. and D. Sześciło. 2016. The benefits and risks of experimental co-production: The case of urban re-design in Vienna. *Public Administration* 94 (2): 509–525.

Bell, S. 2011. Do we really need a new 'constructivist institutionalism' to explain institutional change? *British Journal of Political Science* 41: 883–906.

Bennett, C. J. and M. Howlett. 1992. The lessons of learning: reconciling theories of policy learning and policy change. *Policy Sciences* 25 (3): 275–94.

Bennister, M., P. Worthy and P. 't Hart (eds.). 2017. *The Leadership Capital Index: A New Perspective on Political Leadership*. Oxford: Oxford University Press.

Bevir, M. and R. A. W. Rhodes. 2010. *The State as Cultural Practice*. Oxford: Oxford University Press.

Boje, D. M. 1991a. Consulting and change in the storytelling organisation. *Journal of Organizational Change Management* 4 (3): 7–17.

Boje, D. M. 1991b. The storytelling organization: A story of story performance in an office-supply form. *Administrative Science Quarterly* 36 (1): 106–26.

Bosson, J. K., A. B. Johnson, K. Niederhoffer and W. B. Swann. 2006. Interpersonal chemistry through negativity: Bonding by sharing negative attitudes about others. *Personal Relationships* 13: 135–150.

Boston, J., J. Martin, J. Pallot and P. Walsh. 1996. *Public Management: The New Zealand Model*. Oxford: Oxford University Press.

Boswell, John, Jack Corbett and R. A. W. Rhodes. 2019. *The Art and Craft of Comparison*. Cambridge: Cambridge University Press.

Bouckaert, G. 2017. Taking stock of 'governance': A predominantly European perspective. *Governance* 30 (1): 45–52.

Bovens, M. and P. 't Hart. 1996. *Understanding Policy Fiascos*. New Brunswick, NJ: Transaction Books.

Bovens, M., T. Schillemans and P. 't Hart. 2008. Does public accountability work? An assessment tool. *Public Administration* 86: 225–42.

Brändström, A., F. Bynander and P. 't Hart. 2004. Governing by looking back: Historical analogies and crisis management. *Public Administration* 82 (1): 191–210.

Bruner, J. 1990. *Acts of Meaning*. Cambridge, MA: Harvard University Press.

Cairney, P. 2009. The role of ideas in policy transfer: The case of UK smoking bans since devolution. *Journal of European Public Policy* 16 (3): 471–88.

Cairney, P. 2016. *The Politics of Evidence-Based Policy Making*. London: Palgrave Macmillan.

Carey, G. and B. Crammond. 2015. What works in joined-up government? An evidence synthesis. *International Journal of Public Administration* 38: 1020–1029.

Christensen, T. and P. Lægreid. 2007. The whole-of-government approach to public sector reform. *Public Administration Review* 67 (6): 1059–1066.

Compton, M. and P. 't Hart (eds.). 2019. *Great Policy Successes*. Oxford: Oxford University Press.

Corbett, Jack and Cosmo Howard. 2017. Why perceived size matters for agency termination. *Public Administration* 95 (1): 196–213.

Corbett, Jack, Wouter Veenendaal and John Connell. 2020. The core executive and small states: Is coordination the primary challenge? *Public Administration*. Ahead-of-print DOI: https://doi.org/10.1111/padm.12682

Czarniawska, B. 1997. *Narrating the Organization: Dramas of Institutional Identity*. Chicago, IL: University of Chicago Press.

Czarniawska, B. 2004. *Narratives in Social Science Research*. New York: Sage.

Czarniawska, B. 2017. The Fate of Counter-Narratives: In Fiction and in Actual Organizations. In S. Frandsen, T. Kuhn and M. W. Lundholt (eds.) *Counter-Narratives and Organization*. London: Routledge, 208–226.

Department for Communities and Local Government. 2006. *Building for a Greener Future*.

Department of Industry and Science (Australia). 2015. *Energy White Paper*. https://apo.org.au/sites/default/files/resource-files/2015-04/apo-nid54017.pdf, accessed on 24 September 2020.

Department of Trade and Industry (DTI). 2003. *Our Energy Future – Creating a Low Carbon Economy*. Energy White Paper. https://webarchive .nationalarchives.gov.uk/20090609015453/http://www.berr.gov.uk/files/ file10719.pdf, accessed on 24 September 2020.

Department of State Growth. 2015. *Tasmanian Energy Strategy: Restoring Tasmania's Energy Advantage*. www.stategrowth.tas.gov.au/__data/assets/ pdf_file/0017/100637/Tasmanian_Energy_Strategy_Restoring_Tasmanias_Ene -rgy_Advantage.pdf.pdf, accessed on 24 September 2020.

Duncan, R. B. and A. Weiss. 1979. Organizational Learning: Implications for Organizational Design. In B. M. Staw (ed.) *Research in Organizational Behaviour* (Vol. 1). Greenwich: JAI Press, 75–124.

Dunlop, C. A. 2017. Policy learning and policy failure: Definitions, dimensions and intersections. *Policy and Politics* 45 (1): 3–18.

Dunlop, C. A. and C. M. Radaelli. 2013. Systematising policy learning: From monolith to dimensions. *Political Studies* 61 (3): 599–619.

Elston, T. 2014. Not so 'arm's length': Reinterpreting agencies in UK central government. *Public Administration* 92 (2): 458–76.

Essential Service Commision (ESC) 2004. *Mandatory Rollout of Interval Meters for Electricity Customers: Final Decison*. www.thebackshed.com /forum/uploads/KarlJ/2009-03-08_093433_IMRO_FinalDecisionFinal9July04 .pdf, accessed on 24 September 2020.

Fischer, F. 2003. *Reframing Public Policy: Discursive Politics and Deliberative Practices*. Oxford: Oxford University Press.

Frandsen, S., T. Kuhn and M. W. Lundholt. 2016. Introduction. In S. Frandsen, T. Kuhn and M. W. Lundholt (eds.) *Counter-Narratives and Organization*. London: Routledge, 1–14.

Gaddefors, J. 2007. Metaphor use in the entrepreneurial process. *International Journal of Entrepreneurial Behavior and Research* 13 (3): 173–93.

Gottschall, J. 2012. *The Storytelling Animal: How Stories Make Us Human*. Boston, MA: Houghton Mifflin Harcourt.

Hawley, E., K. Clifford and C. Konkes. 2018. The 'Rosie Batty effect'and the framing of family violence in Australian news media. *Journalism Studies* 19 (15): 2304–2323.

Hay, C. 2011. Interpreting interpretivism interpreting interpretations: The new hermeneutics of public administration. *Public Administration* 89 (1): 167–82.

Head, B. and J. Alford. 2015. Wicked problems: Implications for public policy and management. *Administration and Society* 47 (6): 711–39.

Hendriks, C. M. 2009. The democratic soup: Mixed meanings of political representation in governance networks. *Governance* 22 (4): 689–715.

Hodgman, W. 2015. Family Violence Consultative Group. www .premier.tas.gov.au/releases/family_violence_consultative_group, accessed on 21 December 2019.

Hood, C. 2011. *The Blame Game: Spin, Bureaucracy and Self-Preservation in Government*. Princeton, NJ: Princeton University Press.

Hood, C. and M. Lodge. 2006. *The Politics of Public Service Bargains: Reward, Competency, Loyalty – and Blame*. Oxford: Oxford University Press.

Hope, E. 2015. Premier Will Hodgman declares zero tolerance stance on domestic violence. *The Mercury*, 25 May. www.themercury.com.au/news/tasmania/premier-will-hodgman-declares-zero-tolerance-stance-on-domestic-violence/news-story/64a4c4444ad3bb561e3958c0c962dfbe, accessed on 21 December 2019.

Jensen, K., R. J. Scott, L. Slocombe, R. Boyd and L. Cowey. 2014. The *Management* and *Organisational Challenges* of *More Joined-Up Government*: New Zealand's Better Public Services Reforms. State Sector Performance Hub, Working Paper 2014–1. Wellington: New Zealand Government.

Kane, J. and H. Patapan. 2012. *The Democratic Leader: How Democracy Defines, Empowers, and Limits Its Leaders*. Oxford: Oxford University Press.

King, A. and I. Crewe. 2013. *The Blunders of Our Governments*. London: Oneworld.

Kingdon, J. 1984. *Agendas, Alternatives, and Public Policies*. Boston, MA: Little, Brown & Co.

Kohonen, T. (2012). *Self-Organization and Associative Memory* (Vol. 8).Berlin: Springer Science & Business Media.

Kovecses, Z. (2005). Metaphor: A Practical Introduction. In I. Nonaka (ed.) *Knowledge Management: Critical Perspectives on Business and Management*. New York, NY: Routledge, 101–112.

Lindblom, C. 1959. The science of muddling through. *Public Administration Review* 19 (2): 79–88.

Linde, C. 2009. *Working the Past: Narrative and Institutional Memory*. Oxford: Oxford University Press.

Lindquist, E. A. and C. Eichbaum. 2016. Remaking government in Canada: Dares, resilience and civility in Westminster systems. *Governance* 29 (4): 553–571.

Lovell, H. 2004. Framing sustainable housing as a solution to climate change. *Journal of Environmental Policy and Planning* 6: 35–55.

Lovell, H. 2005. Supply and demand for low energy housing in the UK: Insights from a science and technology studies approach. *Housing Studies* 20 (5): 815–829.

Lovell, H. 2007. Exploring the role of materials in policy change: Innovation in low energy housing in the UK. *Environment and Planning A* 39: 2500–2517.

Lovell, H. 2009. The role of individuals in policy change: The case of UK low energy housing. *Environment and Planning C* 27: 491–511.

Lovell, H. 2017. Are policy failures mobile? An investigation of the Advanced Metering Infrastructure Program in the State of Victoria, Australia. *Environment and Planning A*, 49 (2): 314–331.

Lovell, H. and J. Corbett. 2018. What Makes a Zero Carbon Home Zero Carbon? In R.A.W. Rhodes (ed.) *Narrative Policy Analysis: Cases in Decentred Policy*. London: Palgrave Macmillan, 47–70.

Lowndes, V. and M. Roberts. 2013. *Why Institutions Matter: The New Institutionalism in Political Science*. Basingstoke: Palgrave Macmillan.

McConnell, A. 2010. Policy success, policy failure and grey areas in-between. *Journal of Public Policy* 30 (3): 345–362.

McConnell, A. 2015. What is policy failure? A primer to help navigate the maze. *Public Policy and Administration* 30 (3–4): 221–242.

March, J. G. 1972. Model bias in social action. *Review of Educational Research* 44: 413–429.

March, J. G. 2010. *The Ambiguities of Experience*. Ithaca, NY: Cornell University Press.

Marchment Hill Consulting. 2009. *Victorian AMI Program – Presentation to the National Smart Metering Program, 21st January 2009*. Australian National Smart Metering Program [cited 30th October 2015]. https://link.aemo.com.au /sites/wcl/smartmetering/Document%20library/Smart%20meter%20back ground%20info/Background%20-%20Vic%20AMI%20presentation%20to% 20NSSC%20-%2021%20Jan%202009.pdf, accessed on 24 September 2020.

Marsh, D. 2011. The new orthodoxy: The differentiated polity model. *Public Administration* 89 (1): 32–48.

Marsh, D. and R. A. W. Rhodes. 1992. *Policy Networks in British Government*. Oxford: Clarendon Press.

Nguyen, N. T. and K. Umemoto. 2012. Leading with metaphoric intelligence. *Journal of Leadership Studies* 5 (4): 41–51.

National Smart Metering Program (NSMP). 2008. *National Smart Metering Program Pilots and Trials 2008 Status Report to the Ministerial Council on Energy*. Canberra: NSMP.

NSW Minister for Resources and Energy. 2014. NSW gets smart about meters. Media Release, 28 October. Accessed 24 September 2020. www.anthonyro bertsmp.com.au/media/media-releases/nsw-gets-smart-about-meters, accessed 24 September 2020.

Nystrom, P. C. and W. H. Starbuck. 1984. To avoid organizational crisis, unlearn. *Organizational Dynamics* 12: 53–65.

O'Brien, M. 2011. Smart meters here to stay despite cost blow-out. www.abc .net.au/news/2011-12-14/smart-meter-roll-out-continues-despite-cost-blow-out/3730522, accessed on 9 November 2015.

Osborne, S. (ed.). 2009. *The New Public Governance?* London: Routledge.

Peeters, G. and J. Starbuck 1990. Positive-negative asymmetry in evaluations: The distinction between affective and informational negativity effects. *European Review of Social Psychology* 1: 33–60.

Peters, B. G. 2015. *Advanced Introduction to Public Policy.* Cheltenham: Edward Elgar.

Pierson, P. 2000. Increasing returns, path dependence, and the study of politics. *American Political Science Review* 94 (2): 251–267.

Pierson, P. 2004. *Politics in Time. History, Institutions and Social Analysis.* Princeton, NJ: Princeton University Press.

Pollitt, C. 2000. Institutional amnesia: A paradox of the 'information age'? *Prometheus* 18 (1): 5–16.

Pollitt, C. 2007. Time Out? In K. Schedler and I. Proeller (eds.) *Cultural Aspects of Public Management Reform* (Research in Public Policy Analysis and Management, Vol. 16). Oxford: Emerald Group Publishing Limited, 231–245.

Pollitt, C. 2008. *Time, Policy, Management: Governing With The Past.* Oxford: Oxford University Press.

Pollitt, C. 2009. Bureaucracies remember, post-bureaucratic organizations forget? *Public Administration* 87 (2): 198–218.

Queensland Department of Energy and Water Supply. 2013. *Powering Queensland's Future: The 30-Year Electricity Strategy.* Discussion paper. Brisbane: Queensland Government Department of Energy and Water Supply.

Rhodes, R.A.W. (1996) The new governance: Governing without government. *Political Studies* 44 (4): 652–667.

Rhodes, R. A. W. 1997. *Understanding Governance: Policy Networks, Governance, Reflexivity and Accountability.* Buckingham: Open University Press.

Rhodes, R. A. W. 2011. *Everyday Life in British Government.* Oxford: Oxford University Press.

Rhodes, R. A. W. and A. Tiernan. 2014. *Lessons in Governing. A Profile of Prime Ministers' Chiefs of Staff.* Melbourne: Melbourne University Press.

Rhodes, R. A. W., J. Wanna and P. Weller. 2009. *Comparing Westminster.* Oxford: Oxford University Press.

Richards, D. and M. Smith. 2016. The Westminster model and the 'indivisibility of the political and administrative elite': A convenient myth whose time is up? *Governance* 29 (4): 499–516.

Rittel, H. W. J. and M. M. Webber. 1973. Dilemmas in a general theory of planning. *Policy Sciences* 4 (2): 155–169.

Schick, A. 1996. *The Spirit of Reform.* Wellington: State Services Commission, Government of New Zealand.

Schmidt, V. A. 2008. Discursive institutionalism: The explanatory power of ideas and discourse. *Annual Review of Political Science* 11: 303–326.

Schmidt, V. A. 2010. Taking ideas and discourse seriously: Explaining change through discursive institutionalism as the fourth 'new institutionalism'. *European Political Science Review* 2: 1–25.

Schon, D. A. 1983. *The Reflective Practitioner.* New York: Basic Books.

Scott, R. J. 2019. Explaining how group model building supports enduring agreement. *Journal of Management and Organization* 25 (6): 783–806.

Scott, R. J. and E. Bardach. 2019. A comparison of management adaptations for joined-up government: Lessons from New Zealand. *Australian Journal of Public Administration* 78 (2): 191–212.

Scott, R. J. and R. Boyd. 2015. The New Zealand Better Public Service Results: A Comparative Analysis Linking Inter-agency Collaboration with Outcome Performance. In *Proceedings of the 2015 Australia and New Zealand Academy of Management Conference.* Brisbane: Australia and New Zealand Academy of Management. DOI: 10.13140/RG.2.1.4884.8401.

Scott, R. J. and R. Boyd. 2016a. Joined-up for what? Response to Carey and Harris on adaptive collaboration. *Australian Journal of Public Administration* 76 (1): 138–144.

Scott, R. J. and R. Boyd. 2016b. Results, Targets and Measures to Drive Collaboration: Lessons from the New Zealand Better Public Services reforms. In J. R. Butcher and D. J. Gilchrist (eds.) *The Three Sector Solution: Delivering Public Policy in Collaboration with Not-for-Profits and Business.* Canberra: ANU Press, 235–258.

Scott, R. J. and R. Boyd. 2017. *Interagency Performance Targets: A Case Study of New Zealand's Results Programme.* Washington, DC: IBM Business of Government.

Scott, R. J. and R. Boyd. 2020. Determined to succeed: Can goal commitment sustain interagency collaboration. *Public Policy and Administration.* DOI: https://doi.org/10.1177/0952076720905002.

Scott, R. J., R. Y. Cavana and D. Cameron. 2016. Mechanisms for understanding mental model change in group model building. *Systems Research and Behavioral Science* 33 (1): 100–118.

Scott, R. J. and M. Macaulay. 2020. Making sense of New Zealand's 'spirit of service': Social identity and the civil service. *Public Money and Management.* DOI: 10.1080/09540962.2020.1735109.

Seyfang, G. and A. Smith. 2007. Grassroots innovation for sustainable development: Towards a new research and policy agenda. *Environmental Politics* 16 (4): 584–603.

Smullen, A. 2010. Translating agency reform through durable rhetorical styles: Comparing official agency talk across consensus and adversarial contexts. *Public Administration* 88 (4): 943–959.

St Vincent de Paul Society and Alviss Consulting. 2016. *Households in the Dark: Mapping Electricity Disconnections in South Australia, Victoria, New South Wales and South East Queensland.* Melbourne: St Vincent de Paul Society and Alviss Consulting.

Star, S. L. and J. R. Griesemer. 1989. Institutional ecology, 'translations' and boundary objects: Amateurs and professionals in Berkeley's Museum of Vertebrate Zoology, 1907–39. *Social Studies of Science* 19 (3): 387–420.

Stark, A. 2019. Explaining institutional amnesia in government. *Governance* 32 (1): 143–158.

Stark, A. and B. Head. 2019. Institutional amnesia and public policy. *Journal of European Public Policy* 26 (10): 1521–1539.

Stone, D. 2012. *Policy Paradox: The Art of Political Decision Making.* London and New York: W.W. Norton & Co.

Sullivan, H. 2015. Democracy and hybrid governance in Australia. *Meanjin* 74 (3): 120–122.

TasNetworks. 2015. Expanding competition in metering and related services (ERC0169). TasNetworks submission to AEMC Consultation on Draft Rule.

Tsoukas, H. 1991. The missing link: A transformational view of metaphor in organizational science. *Academy of Management Review* 16 (3): 566–585.

Toke, D. 2000. Policy network creation: The case of energy efficiency. *Public Administration* 78 (4): 835–854.

't Hart, P. 2014. *Understanding Public Leadership.* London: Palgrave Macmillan.

Victorian Auditor-General's Office (VAGO). 2015. *Realising the Benefits of Smart Meters.* Melbourne: Victorian Auditor-General's Office.

Victorian State Government. 2015. Smart meters. www.smartmeters.vic.gov.au /about-smart-meters/government-review, accessed 30 October 2015.

Walsh, J. P. and G. R. Ungson. 1991. Organizational memory. *Academy of Management Review* 16 (1): 57–91.

Wettenhall, R. 2011. Organisational amnesia: A serious public sector reform issue. *International Journal of Public Sector Management* 24 (1): 80–96.

White, H. 1973. *Metahistory: The Historical Imagination in Nineteenth-Century Europe.* Baltimore, MD: Johns Hopkins University.

Acknowledgments

We would like to thank all of our interviewees across the four cases who gave so freely and openly of their time to make this research possible. The Australia and New Zealand School of Government (ANZSOG) provided the funding for this research and *Governance* gave permission to republish an amended version of our article (Jack Corbett, Dennis C. Grube, Heather Lovell and Rodney Scott (2018), "Singular memory or institutional memories? Toward a dynamic approach," *Governance* 31 (3): 555–573) as the introduction to this Element. We owe a debt to anonymous reviewers at both Cambridge University Press and *Governance* for generous comments that helped us improve the text. We have greatly appreciated the professionalism of the editors of Elements in Public and Nonprofit Administration and the production team at Cambridge University Press as we finalised the manuscript. Heather Lovell would also like to thank the Australian Research Council, which part funded the Victorian Smart Meter case under its Future Fellowship Programme – Project ID FT140100646. Rodney Scott would like to thank Ngaire Woods and the Blavatnik School of Government for hosting his 2018 Fellowship. Jack Corbett would like to thank Dave Marsh for getting him thinking about institutional memory. We would all like to acknowledge colleagues at our respective institutions (Cambridge, Griffith, Tasmania, Southampton and the University of New South Wales) for their wisdom and insight. Finally, as ever, this book would not have been possible without the love and support of our nearest and dearest.

Cambridge Elements ≡

Public and Nonprofit Administration

Andrew Whitford
University of Georgia
Andrew Whitford is Alexander M. Crenshaw Professor of Public Policy in the School of Public and International Affairs at the University of Georgia. His research centers on strategy and innovation in public policy and organization studies.

Robert Christensen
Brigham Young University
Robert Christensen is professor and George Romney Research Fellow in the Marriott School at Brigham Young University. His research focuses on prosocial and antisocial behaviors and attitudes in public and nonprofit organizations.

About the Series
The foundation of this series are cutting-edge contributions on emerging topics and definitive reviews of keystone topics in public and nonprofit administration, especially those that lack longer treatment in textbook or other formats. Among keystone topics of interest for scholars and practitioners of public and nonprofit administration, it covers public management, public budgeting and finance, nonprofit studies, and the interstitial space between the public and nonprofit sectors, along with theoretical and methodological contributions, including quantitative, qualitative and mixed-methods pieces.

The Public Management Research Association
The Public Management Research Association improves public governance by advancing research on public organizations, strengthening links among interdisciplinary scholars, and furthering professional and academic opportunities in public management.

Cambridge Elements ≡

Public and Nonprofit Administration

Elements in the Series

Motivating Public Employees
Marc Esteve and Christian Schuster

Organizational Obliviousness: Entrenched Resistance to Gender Integration in the Military
Alesha Doan and Shannon Portillo

Partnerships that Last: Identifying the Keys to Resilient Collaboration
Heather Getha-Taylor

Behavioral Public Performance: How People Make Sense of Government Metrics
Oliver James, Donald P. Moynihan, Asmus Leth Olsen and Gregg G. Van Ryzin

Redefining Development: Resolving Complex Challenges in Developing Countries
Jessica Kritz

Gender, Risk and Leadership: The Glass Cliff in Public Service Careers
Leisha DeHart-Davis, Deneen Hatmaker, Kim Nelson, Sanjay K. Pandey, Sheela Pandey and Amy Smith

Institutional Memory as Storytelling: How Networked Government Remembers
Jack Corbett, Dennis C. Grube, Heather Lovell, Rodney James Scott

A full series listing is available at: www.cambridge.org/EPNP

Lightning Source UK Ltd.
Milton Keynes UK
UKHW021302240121
377557UK00007B/114